55 MEN
THE STORY
OF THE CONSTITUTION

55 MEN
THE STORY OF
THE CONSTITUTION

Based on the
day-by-day notes of
James Madison

by
Fred Rodell, *1907–*

Stackpole Books

Copyright © 1936 by The Telegraph Press

First paperback edition, 1986, Stackpole Books

Published by
STACKPOLE BOOKS
Cameron and Kelker Streets
P.O. Box 1831
Harrisburg, PA 17105

Printed in the U.S.A.

Library of Congress Cataloging-in-Publication Data

Rodell, Fred, 1907–
    55 men: story of the constitution.

    1. United States—Constitutional history.
2. United States. Constitutional Convention (1787)
3. Madison, James, 1751–1836.   I. Title.   II. Title:
Fifty-five men.
KF4541.R63   1986   342.73′0292   86-5794
ISBN 0-8117-2171-X   347.302292

To
The School Children
and
The Politicians—
for the same reason

CONTENTS

FOREWORD

On September 17, 1987, the United States will celebrate the 200th anniversary of the completion of the convention in Philadelphia that drafted the Constitution. It is likely that that day will be declared a national holiday and that the leaders of the country will gather in Philadelphia for a nationally televised celebration of this important anniversary. But unlike the Bicentennial of the Declaration of Independence or even the 100th birthday of the Statue of Liberty, the Bicentennial of the Constitution of the United States is not well suited to tall ships and soaring fireworks. The Constitution was a triumph of the mind. Its anniversary is best celebrated by educating the American people about how the Constitution came into existence and how it affects our lives today.

To this process Stackpole Books has made an important contribution by republishing Fred Rodell's *55 Men*. This book, which has long been out of print, is a splendidly readable and lucid account of the Constitutional Convention. The events of the summer of 1787 come vividly to life in Rodell's telling of them. His account is based primarily on the notes James Madison kept of the convention, but Rodell presents the information contained in the notes in a lively and atmospheric way. The book is dedicated: "To The School Children and The Politicians—for the same reason." Both can read it with enjoyment and with profit. I was in junior high school when I first read the book. I learned from it then, and re-reading it now, after teaching Constitutional Law for more than 30 years, I found that I learned from it again.

These 55 men from 12 states (Rhode Island did not send any delegates) had been gathered to make some minor changes in the Articles of Confederation, but they quickly decided to draft a wholly new document, a Constitution that would establish a strong national government. Since there was no precedent for what they were doing, it is hardly surprising that they stumbled and vacillated. Should there be one President or three? How should that officer be chosen? Should the Supreme Court be elected by Congress? Should Congressmen be eligible for reelection? On these and many other issues the delegates fumbled. We idolize them today and speak of them as "the Framers" or "the Founding Fathers," and surely we were fortunate that among them were so many men of wisdom and common sense. Even so, as this book shows, they were not supermen, and many of the provisions of the Constitution got there by compromise or through a long process of trying one idea after another and finally choosing the solution that seemed to have the fewest defects.

There were important differences between the large states and the small, though it is interesting to see that Virginia, Massachusetts, and Pennsylvania were the three largest states and that New York consistently voted with the small states. There were differences, largely but not wholly because of slavery, between the northern and the southern states. Even here, however, the states had their own interests and were not merely part of a bloc. When the states of the deep South wanted to write into the Constitution a provision barring Congress from interfering with the importation of slaves, delegates from Maryland and Virginia opposed this, and made righteous comments about the evils of the slave trade. This was too much for Oliver Ellsworth of Connecticut, who remarked that "slaves multiply so fast in Virginia and Maryland that it is cheaper to raise than import them." He pointed out also that if importation of slaves were stopped, the states in the deep South, where the death rate of slaves was higher, would have to purchase slaves from Virginia and Maryland. This is the sort of illuminating incident that is now largely lost in the mists of history.

It is somewhat staggering to think that it is now 50 years since *55 Men* was originally published. Much has happened since. The whole course of constitutional interpretation was changed dramatically in 1937, when the Supreme Court, which had been striking down New Deal legislation and similar attempts by the states to cope with the trauma of the Depression, reversed itself and left it to Congress and state legislatures to decide whether and how business is to be regulated. In 1936 civil rights did not much figure in Supreme Court decisions. Today much of the Court's work is in interpreting the Bill of Rights and the other provisions in the Constitution and its amendments that protect individual liberty.

There have been other kinds of changes as well in the half century since this book first appeared. New historical research has shown that the published version of the convention notes of Robert Yates, a delegate from New York, which has been one of our lesser sources of information about what went on behind the closed door of the convention, was substantially rewritten for political purposes and must be regarded as worthless. There is even significant question now about the authenticity of the Madison notes on which Rodell principally relies. There have also been new views on how the historical record should be understood; the economic interpretation that Rodell presents, that the delegates were primarily interested in protecting the propertied interests against the poor, is more disputed now than it was in 1936. But these differences, though of great importance to scholars, do not affect the value of *55 Men*. The large picture, as Rodell presents it, is not likely to be changed.

There has been one other change since 1936. Fred Rodell was a 28-year-old assistant professor at the Yale Law School when this book was published. He died in 1980, after he retired as a Yale professor. He was my friend, and I have said elsewhere what I thought about him. [Wright, *Goodbye to Fred Rodell*, 89 Yale L.J. 1455 (1980)] As Fred's friend, I welcome the reappearance of this book, but I welcome it even more in my role as a member of the Commission on the Bicentennial of the United States Constitution. There is no better way to celebrate the anniversary of the Constitution than by reading a book such as this, which presents so interesting and enlightening an account of how the Constitution came into being.

> *Charles Alan Wright*
> *Bates Chair for the Administration*
> *of Justice*
> *The University of Texas Law School*

March, 1986

PREFACE

So many myths and mists have somehow come to settle around the figures of the Founding Fathers, that I think it best to make one thing clear right at the start. The story of the Constitutional Convention, as told in these pages, comes straight from the day-to-day notes James Madison took at that Convention, not quite a hundred and fifty years ago.

The quoted statements of the delegates are copied word for word from Madison. Once in a while, I have changed the form of a verb or pronoun, in order to turn his indirect quotation into a direct one. To anyone who, for his own purpose, may accuse me of citing scripture for my purpose, I can only answer that I have no purpose—save to tell the story as it really happened. To any honest doubter, I can only say, in all sincerity: Go read Madison's notes yourself.

Occasionally, I have also used the more fragmentary notes kept by a few other delegates to the Convention. And for parts of the opening chapter and a bit of the next to last one, I am in debt—as must everyone who writes of those times be in debt—to the work of Dr. Charles A. Beard, dean of American historians. But my chief debt, of course, is to the shade of Mr. Madison.

Fred Rodell

New Haven,
February, 1936

I

THEY KNEW WHAT THEY WANTED

THERE were no airplanes, no railroads, no four-lane concrete highways in those days. They came to Philadelphia on horse and by stage-coach over narrow dirt roads, or aboard ships that needed wind in their sails to make them go. From the great plantations of the South and from the bustling cities of New England they came, these men who were to build in a written document—and hand written, for there were no typewriters—the foundation of the United States.

They had planned to meet on the fourteenth of May. But travel was so slow and uncertain in 1787 that it was not until Friday the twenty-fifth, almost two weeks later, that enough of them had reached Philadelphia to let the Convention get under way. Even then, only twenty-nine members had arrived. And for weeks men from the farther states up and down the Atlantic seaboard kept straggling into town, until finally fifty-five of them, representing twelve of the thirteen states, had taken their seats.

Only little Rhode Island refused to send down delegates. Jealous of its powers as an independent state, afraid that under a national government of any kind the larger states would take away those powers, it decided to keep a wary hands-off. And for more than three years after the Constitution was written, little Rhode Island stuck to its guns, refusing to have any part of the new government until at length it was literally forced by circumstances to become the last of the original states to join the Union.

And of the men appointed by the other states, seven felt as strongly as did Rhode Island about the dangers of national power and declined to take their places at Philadelphia. One of the seven was Patrick Henry, who saw in the business of the Convention a threat to the liberty he prized so highly.

But George Washington was there, representing Virginia; and others, as respected then as they are famous now. There were the Morrises, Gouverneur and Robert, speaking for Pennsylvania. There were Oliver Ellsworth and Roger Sherman from Connecticut. South Carolina sent the Pinckneys and John Rutledge. Alexander Hamilton talked for New York. James Madison and Edmund Randolph joined General Washington from Virginia. John Dickinson represented Delaware. Massachusetts sent Elbridge Gerry and Rufus King. And Benjamin Franklin whom the other members

14

reverently called "Doctor," eighty-one years old but still young in spirit, attended the sessions as often as his health would allow.

Among those who met in Philadelphia were eight who had signed the Declaration of Independence eleven years before. Its author, Thomas Jefferson, was not one of them. He was abroad in Paris, acting as minister to France, at the time. And there are many who think that the Constitution might be a different document had he sat in the Convention that framed it. For Jefferson was one of the men who later insisted that the powers originally given the national government be softened by adding to the Constitution the Bill of Rights, as the first ten amendments are often called.

Unknown of course to themselves or the others, there sat in the Convention two future presidents of the nation they were founding. A future vice-president was also there. And five future members of the Supreme Court, two of whom were to become chief justices, helped write the Court into the Constitution. Judged by their activities both before and after they met in Philadelphia, the Convention was made up of a remarkable group of public men.

Strangely enough, they had not officially come together to set down a Constitution. They

15

had been sent by their states only to make a few changes in the flimsy Articles of Confederation, under which the states had been working as a sort of thirteen-man team since they had won their independence from England. Most of the delegates had been carefully warned that they had no right to do any more than amend the Articles. And any changes made, no matter how slight, were to be agreed to by each of the states themselves, through their legislatures, before they went into effect.

Under the Articles of Confederation there was really no national government at all. There was a Congress in which, as in the Senate today, each of the states had equal voting power. Each state, in other words, no matter how large or how small, had one vote. And that Congress was the only official body that kept the thirteen states together.

There was no separate president, no vice-president, no cabinet, no real executive officer of any kind. There were no federal courts of law. The Congress could pass laws but it had no way of enforcing them. That was up to the states which in turn, if they did not like what Congress did, had only to pay no attention to it.

The Congress could vote to use money for some national purpose. But it could not, on its

16

own hook, get the money to use. The money had to be supplied, if at all, by gifts from the state treasuries. Or if the money was borrowed from private citizens, then it could not be repaid until the state legislatures voted Congress the funds to repay it.

The Congress could declare war. But it could not fight a war unless the states supplied men. It could not regulate money or trade, it could not enforce foreign treaties, it could not push back the Indians on the Western frontier, without the consent and voluntary aid of the separate states themselves. The members of this ridiculously helpless Congress were even paid not out of a national fund, but by the states that sent them.

This Congress, which was all there was of a federal government, was really not much more than an interstate conference. Its set-up was surprisingly like that of the League of Nations today. Each state was bound only so far as it wanted to be bound. Concerted action could be taken only when enough states felt like taking that action separately.

* The fact that the central government had no teeth was reflected in the business conditions of the times. To the big land-owners it made very little difference. But the merchants and

17

manufacturers and bankers, the men with money invested and money to invest, missed the strong helping hand of a national government.

They missed it in several ways. In the first place, many of them held continental bonds, the bonds issued to get money to pay for the Revolution. Some of the holders had loaned the money themselves. Others had bought the bonds cheap, or had bought the certificates issued to the soldiers to pay them for fighting the War. These bonds and certificates were selling for as low as one-twentieth of their face value. The federal government's promise to pay one hundred dollars was considered worth as little as five dollars. For the government had no way of paying interest on its debts, much less the debts themselves.

There was some effort made to pay off these debts in Western lands. But here, too, the hand of a strong government was missed. For the frontier territory was almost worthless unless it was cleared and protected against the danger of Indian raids. This the Confederation could not do. And the states hesitated to take on the job, feeling that it was more a national task and that somehow, some time, the central government might undertake it—and pay for it.

So those who had invested in Western land,

18

along with those who had got it in exchange for paper promises, bemoaned the lack of a government strong enough to clear the frontier. They saw in such a government their only hope of making money out of what seemed just then a very bad investment.

Then the manufacturers, centered mostly in New England, missed the protective tariff wall that a national government might build for them. Without it, they were forced to sell their wares in competition with cheaper goods imported from the old-established shops and mills of Europe. And when they in turn tried to sell their products across the water, they were met with tariff duties that made foreign markets impossible.

The lack of foreign markets made the shipping interests, too, miss a strong central government, a government that might raise its own tariff walls and then bargain with other countries to lower theirs. The shipping interests also missed a national navy to protect merchant-ships flying the American flag.

The handicaps in the path of the manufacturers threw their shadow, in turn, on the lot of the working man. He found jobs scarcer and wages lower. He too, though not so well aware of it as his bosses, missed the advantages that a

19

national government could give to all industry.

Finally the money-lenders, the men who held private notes and mortgages, were cruelly in need of a central control over the currency. The state legislatures were largely in the hands of, or at least influenced by, the debtor groups— the small farmers and others who owed money. State laws were being passed, postponing or reducing payments, issuing cheap paper money as legal tender—laws to relieve the debtors at the expense of their creditors. Since the state governments were supreme, the creditors were helpless. Their choice was to accept, often belatedly, a small part of what was owed them, or to get nothing.

In Massachusetts a debtor group, not satisfied with what it could get by law, had broken out into armed revolt. Here, too, was a sign of something to be feared so long as there was no central government strong enough to help the states squelch riots and rebellion.

Under the Articles of Confederation, it had been the small farmers and the ever-growing debtor class who had fared the best. The state legislatures were pretty much under their control. No wonder then that they tried to tie the hands of the men they sent to the Convention in Philadelphia. No wonder they made it painfully clear that they would accept no more than a slight revision of the Articles. They did not want to lose, under a strong national government, the upper hand that they held in the separate states.

But the men who put the Convention across had different ideas. They had seen one convention, called for Annapolis the year before, break up in failure. Only five of the thirteen states had sent delegates. The rest had been frightened off by the mere suggestion of strengthening the central government.

So this time the men who wanted a Convention were more cautious. They sent out a call to the states for delegates. The call, warily worded by Alexander Hamilton, made the whole plan sound as harmless as possible. All that was wanted was to make a few minor changes in the Articles of Confederation. Even these changes, after they were made, were to go back to the states, which could then decide whether or not they wanted to accept them.

The states—all except cagey little Rhode Island—could not object to this. Treating the whole business almost casually, they appointed their delegates. And for the most part, these delegates were the men who had worked for the Convention, and who now put themselves forth

21

as candidates and were accepted almost as a matter of course.

It is a mistake to think of these men as visionary dreamers, playing around at Philadelphia with abstract conceptions of political theory, pulling a whole scheme of government out of the air like a rabbit out of a hat. True, many of them had read and studied enough about the science of politics to put the average statesman of today to shame. But political science was to them an extremely practical topic of discussion, dealing with the extremely practical business of running a government—not, as today, a branch of higher learning reserved for the use of graduate students.

They were essentially hard-headed men of affairs. Almost all of them were wealthy or well-to-do. They and their friends were among those who missed most the hand of a strong national government. They knew what such a government could do for business, in many ways. And they believed that only under such a government, capable and willing to protect business and trade and property from the dangers that threatened on every side, could the new nation grow.

So they came to Philadelphia with their tongues somewhat in their cheeks. It did not take them long to untie the knots with which the states thought their hands were safely bound. The knots had been nothing but slip-knots all the time.

Unquestionably, these men went far beyond the limits that the states which sent them there intended to put on them. Inasmuch as they did so, it might perhaps be said that the writing of the Constitution was unconstitutional. The job they were given to do was to change the Articles of Confederation.

But when they went back to their homes, after working and debating through four long months of a hot Philadelphia summer, they had done a great deal more. They had set down on paper the foundation of the United States.

* * * *

The first business before the Convention on its first day was the choosing of a president. Robert Morris nominated George Washington. There were no other nominations.

To get some small idea of what the other members thought of Washington, imagine General Pershing, John D. Rockefeller, and Charles A. Lindbergh all rolled into one person today. For Washington, as well as having led the American forces to victory in the Revolution, was the richest, the best known, the most ad-

23

mired citizen of his time.

As Madison scribbled in his notes after Morris finished his speech: "The nomination came with particular grace from Pennsylvania, as Doctor Franklin alone could have been thought of as a competitor. The Doctor was himself to have made the nomination of General Washington, but the state of the weather and of his health confined him to his house."

The election was unanimous. The man who was to become the nation's first president took the chair to preside over the meeting which created that nation. Not being an old hand at this sort of job—he was, after all, used to a more active life—he apologized for his inexperience and hoped he would not make too many mistakes. Then a committee was appointed to draw up rules for the Convention and the members adjourned for the week-end.

The rules, adopted the following Monday, show how seriously these men went about their work. One of the rules required that "Every member, rising to speak, shall address the President; and whilst he shall be speaking, none shall pass between them, or hold discourse with another, or read a book, pamphlet or paper, printed or manuscript—." The impressive and business-like air that must have hung over an assembly, where this rule was rigidly enforced and followed, makes a queer contrast with the casual or else riotous scene that is often enacted on the floor of Congress today.

Today, also, any such meeting as this would have its flock of newspaper reporters jotting down notes, interviewing members, rushing their stories off by phone or telegraph. Tomorrow's papers would carry streamer headlines and syndicated features by special writers. Important speeches would be broadcast over a national network.

But the Constitutional Convention ruled that its deliberations should be kept strictly secret; "That nothing spoken in the House be printed, or otherwise published or communicated without leave."

These men felt that they had come together, not to make speeches, but to get things done. They did not want publicity of any sort. It is said that when Benjamin Franklin, good-natured and garrulous, went out at night to dinner, a close-mouthed member was always at his side to see that the old gentleman did not talk too freely.

Even in the official minutes of the Convention, kept by its secretary, none of the discussion, none of the debates were set down. Nothing but

25

the formal motions themselves and the lists of ayes and noes were put on record. And even that record was closed to outsiders until the Convention was over.

But James Madison, sitting with his back to Washington, facing the other members, made himself the real reporter of the Convention. Day in and day out he sat there, writing down in a sort of makeshift short-hand the debates, the speeches, everything that went on.

The other members, knowing of course what he was doing, knowing that they could trust him for both accuracy and secrecy, gave him their silent approval. They helped him fill out his notes with their own copies or memories of what they had said. And it was not until after Madison, the last living member of the Convention, had died, that his notes were published.

It is only in these notes of Madison's that there exists today any nearly complete record of what really happened back in 1787, when fifty-five men from twelve young states got together in Philadelphia and hammered out a Constitution.

II

DEMOCRACY IN DISGRACE

IT was Edmund Randolph, then Governor of Virginia although he was still in his early thirties, who opened the main business of the Convention by presenting a plan for a national government. It was the same Edmund Randolph who, on the last day of the Convention, refused to sign the finished Constitution because it was so different from that plan, which he had helped to draw up, and had originally set forth.

In between came long weeks of argument and counter-argument, open debate and secret conference, hashing and rehashing of every point in the plan. Randolph's suggestions were torn apart and made over, changed and changed back again five or six times. They were considered and re-considered, elaborated and amended, and countless provisions were added. Yet all the debates, the compromises, and the changes stemmed from those first suggestions. It was out of the Randolph plan that the finished Constitution grew.

The plan itself was not in the form of a constitution. It was a series of resolutions, setting up the bare framework of a national government. And that framework was strangely like

29

and yet strangely unlike the form of the federal government today.

There was to be, as today, a legislature made up of two branches, and one of the branches was to be elected by the people. The legislature was of course to make the national laws. There was also to be an executive branch of the government to carry out the laws; and there were to be national courts to help enforce them. No more of those futile law-making gestures, as under the Confederation. In short, the government was to be divided, as it is today, into three branches, each with its own duties and its own powers. But there the likeness ends.

Although the House of Representatives was to be elected by the people, the Senate in turn was to be elected by the House. Then in both houses of Congress, the number of representatives allowed to each state was to depend not only on its population but also on the wealth of its citizens as measured by the amount of taxes they paid. No doubt New York and the other richer states would give a great deal to see that clause in the Constitution today.

Congressmen were to be ineligible for a second term, so that the whole House would change its membership at every election. And even during their short terms these Congressmen could be recalled from office if the voters did not approve what they were doing.

The powers of Congress were not, as they are today, put down in black and white in the plan —with one exception. That exception was the absolute right to veto any and all laws passed by the separate states. Randolph was not taking any chances with those paper money statutes.

The national executive was to be elected, not by the people, not by electors chosen by the people, but by Congress itself. And that Congress-elected executive was not to be one man, like the president today. Although the plan did not specify one way or the other, Randolph later made it very clear that he was afraid a single president would in time become a tyrannical monarch. What he meant by an executive was a council of three men.

Moreover, these three men were not to enjoy by themselves, as does the president today, a veto power over Congress. The Supreme Court was to join with them in vetoing national laws. So the Supreme Court veto in turn was not to come, as it does today, in decisions made long after the laws were passed—but immediately, before the laws went into effect. On the other hand, this quick Supreme Court veto could be overruled, as it can not be today, by another and

31

stronger vote of Congress in favor of the vetoed law.

When Randolph had finished reading his resolutions, the Convention decided that the proper way to handle them was to turn them over to a committee. But since the resolutions contained in themselves the seed of the whole work of the Convention, it did not seem fair to exclude any of the members from the privilege of considering them first-hand. So the Convention turned itself into a committee of the whole. And for three weeks the entire membership discussed and argued, as a committee, the same propositions which the same men were to discuss and argue all over again after the committee had made its report to the Convention.

The first question to be decided was whether a real government with three branches, a national government with teeth, was to be substituted for the doddering Confederation. This was of course the biggest problem of all. Yet now there was almost no discussion. The delegates seemed to take it for granted that they were there to disobey the orders their states had given them. It is true that, as though they were heralding at that early date the Southern tradition of states' rights, the two Pinckneys from South Carolina rose—the one to ask if this would mean abolishing the states, the other to doubt the power of the Convention to go so far. But a few minutes later, South Carolina's vote joined the chorus of ayes.

One of the first changes made in Randolph's plan was in his set-up of the national executive. Over his strong objections it was argued that putting three men in the presidency together would mean endless squabbles, red tape, and delay in the carrying out of laws. Moreover, there was more danger of tyranny from three men than from one—and yet one would be more likely to stand on his own feet, independent of Congress.

It was even suggested at one point that, since Congress was then to elect the executive, Congress should be allowed to put in any number of men it thought best, whether one or twenty-one. But when James Wilson pointed out that the thirteen states, "tho agreeing in scarce any other instance," all used one man for governor, it was voted that the nation should follow their example and elect one president.

How this president was to be elected remained a constant trouble-maker, and was not finally decided until the Convention was almost over. But the notion of having more than one president was not raised again. And the wisdom of

33

this early choice is pretty clearly indicated by imagining the confusion today if, say, Hoover, Roosevelt, and Al Smith were now joint presidents.

* Since there was to be, then, a one-man president, what good would it do to give him his veto power along with the Supreme Court, who could so easily outvote him? Elbridge Gerry thought the Supreme Court should be kept out of it. The judges, he said, would probably get their chance later to declare laws unconstitutional.

But Madison was strong for letting the judges in at the beginning. He thought the president, in vetoing laws, would need plenty of moral support, particularly—with a canny prediction— since the president in office "will be envied and assailed by disappointed competitors." On the other hand, Gerry answered, it was more likely that, instead of receiving support, the president would be "seduced by the sophistry of the judges." So it was decided, for the time being, that the president should exercise his veto alone.

Should the veto, then, to give the president strength, be an absolute one—with Congress having no power at all to overrule it? Colonel Mason thought this would give the president too much of an upper hand and too much chance to abuse it. He could hold up all the laws until

Congress agreed to any appointments he wanted to make.

No, replied Wilson and Alexander Hamilton, with a very bad guess—the veto power will hardly ever be used. For instance, King George over in England has not used his veto power since the Revolution.

At this point Benjamin Franklin entered the argument, and settled it. Look at Pennsylvania, he said, if you want an example. There a few years back, "the Indians were scalping the western people" out around the Alleghenies, and the governor refused to send troops out to fight them until the legislature had agreed to exempt him from all taxes. Whereupon, the Convention agreed to let the president's veto be overruled by a two-thirds vote of Congress.

But Randolph's proposal to let Congress veto all laws passed by the states was not disposed of so easily. Madison was its chief champion. He thought it "absolutely necessary" to give the national government control over the states. Without it, the government would have to resort to force to keep the upper hand.

Immediate protest came from the spokesmen for the smaller states. They were sure that the large states, with more votes in Congress, would "crush" the business and industry of the small

35

ones. Here was the first real display of state pride, looking out for the pocketbook of some of the small states' citizens.

But even those who feared that Congress, if given the power to veto state laws, would use that veto power unfairly, were perfectly willing to see that veto used on "paper money and similar measures." If it were so limited, they would not object to it. It would no longer offend their state pride.

Then, some of the lawyers present pointed out that any really bad state laws, like the bad national laws, would be called unconstitutional by the courts. So the right of Congress to veto state laws was voted down. But only after Madison had once more risen to plead that, by the time the courts got around to throwing out bad laws, the damage would already be done.

And weeks later, Pinckney and Madison, still not satisfied, raised the point again. This time, Colonel Mason made the very sensible comment that it would be a tremendous waste of time to make Congress go over every single law that any state might pass. If "no road nor bridge is to be established without the sanction of the general legislature," Congress would have to stay in session continually and do nothing but look over state laws. And John Rutledge, peeved at the persistence of some of his colleagues, shouted that "this alone would damn and ought to damn the Constitution." The motion was quickly and finally withdrawn.

Yet, disputes such as this were minor ones. It was over the setting up of Congress that the real trouble started. Before it subsided, the delegates were divided into two camps at swords' points, and the Convention had threatened to break up in complete failure. And though the question of how the states should be represented in Congress was the fuse that set off the big explosion, the question of how members of Congress should be elected brought on some preliminary fire-works.

In the Randolph plan, the people were to elect the House of Representatives and nothing more. They were to have no say in choosing the Senate nor the judges nor the president, whether one or three. And yet, in the Convention, there was strong objection to giving the people even so small a voice in the national government.

No sooner was Randolph's proposition read than Roger Sherman demanded election of the House by the state legislatures. He felt that "the people should have as little to do as may be about the government. They want information and are constantly liable to be misled."

Pinckney came out with the real reason for this mistrust of a popular election. "A majority of the people in South Carolina," he said, "are notoriously for paper-money as a legal tender." And he added that election by the state legislatures "would be a better guard against bad measures."

On the other hand, many of those who favored a popular election did so only because they feared the legislatures more than the people. Gerry admitted "the evils we experience flow from the excess of democracy." Yet he felt that "in Massachusetts the worst men get into the legislature." And Rufus King, also from Massachusetts, agreed with him that there lay greater danger in an election of the House by the legislatures, who "would constantly choose men subservient to their own views" favoring paper money laws.

Moreover, Gerry added, as though throwing a sop to the people, they had better elect one branch of the government "in order to inspire them with the necessary confidence." And Mason, too, conceded that "whatever inconveniency may attend the democratic principle, it must actuate one part of the government."

Finally, Madison chimed in with a desire "to

provide more effectually for the security of private rights," and yet somehow keep "consistent with the democratic form of government." He felt, though, that the strength of a popular majority could be broken up by scattering it over a wider territory. And the fact that, in national elections, the voters would be spread throughout thirteen states would thus prove "the only defence against the inconveniences of democracy."

⁎It may amaze those who learned their American history from the average sixth-grade textbook to hear the founding fathers speaking of democracy so harshly. Yet, much as it sounds like sacrilege, these men had no cause to be overfond of democracy as they knew it. They were, after all, almost without exception, men of affairs. The democracy they knew was the democracy that burdened their trade and their business with high taxes, reduced the value of their bonds and securities, and kept them from collecting the debts that were owed them. It was the democracy practiced in the separate states at the time.

And, not only in the debates over the election of Congress, but throughout the Convention, the members continued to express their dislike and their fear of popular government. Gerry spoke of "the ignorance of the people" and of "the danger of the levelling spirit." Again, he re-

39

marked that the people in New England, "have the wildest ideas of government in the world."

Gouverneur Morris insisted that "the people never act from reason alone," and called them "the dupes of those who have more knowledge." Randolph thought "the evils under which the U. S. labors" had their origin "in the turbulence and follies of democracy."

Hamilton referred to the "vices" and again to the "imprudence of democracy;" and commented that "the people seldom judge or determine right." And Mason said it would be as bad to let the people elect a president "as it would to refer a trial of colours to a blind man."

In the face of sentiments such as these, it was pretty clear that the people were not going to be given the election of the Senate. They had been handed the privilege of choosing the House, for a variety of reasons—of which enthusiasm for democracy was not one. The general feeling in the Convention was that the Senate ought to be picked in such a way as to make it a safe-and-sane check on any wild ideas coming from the democratic House.

Randolph had proposed that the House itself elect the Senate, thus removing the choice at least one step from the people. The plan never got much support. It was not likely that the

40

House would put men into the Senate who would fight against the House's own schemes.

Read of Delaware wanted the Senate appointed by the president—a frank step in the direction of monarchy. But the Senate, at that point in the deliberations, was to help elect the president—and the combination might h a v e proved slightly confusing.

From the beginning, there was pretty general agreement on the plan finally adopted, namely, election of the Senate by the state legislatures. True, James Wilson—more than a century ahead of his time—argued valiantly for election by the people. And Madison gave him occasional support.

But, as Madison himself admitted, there were cross-currents at work here. For it was taken for granted that the Senate was going to be small. And election by the state legislatures meant that each state would have at least one senator. And if each state was to have at least one senator and the Senate was to be small, that meant that the larger states could not be represented in the Senate in proportion to their size.

Wilson was from Pennsylvania. Madison was from Virginia. Virginia, Pennsylvania, and Massachusetts were—and were constantly referred to at the Convention as—the Big Three

41

among the states. So when Wilson and Madison talked against election of the Senate by the state legislatures, they were not exactly giving the people a vote of confidence.

Moreover, their opponents from the smaller states were well aware of this. Arguing that the states themselves, through their legislatures, ought to help choose Congress, Ellsworth of Connecticut added quite gratuitously: "The largest states are the worst governed. Virginia is obliged to acknowledge her incapacity to extend her government to Kentuckey. Massachusetts cannot keep the peace one hundred miles from her capitol. How long Pennsylvania may be free from a like situation cannot be foreseen."

Yet underneath these early exchanges of pleasantries there again ran a current of agreement. Gerry, although from Massachusetts, wanted the Senate elected by the legislatures because "the commercial and moneyed interest would be more secure in their hands." "To draw both branches from the people," he said, "will leave no security to the commercial interest including the stockholders." Dickinson of Delaware, for the same reason, hoped for a Senate "distinguished for their rank in life and their weight of property, and bearing as strong a likeness to the British House of Lords as possible."

42

But Wilson, arguing on the other side, insisted it was the legislatures that "now sacrifice the commercial to the landed interest." And Madison, backing him up, added that "the great evils complained of are that the state legislatures run into schemes of paper money. Nothing can be more contradictory than to say that the national legislature without a proper check will follow the example of the state legislatures, and in the same breath, that the state legislatures are the only proper check."

In short, the spokesmen for both sides, whether from large states or small, were at bottom after the same result—protection against paper money and similar popular laws. And in the end, when the votes were counted, they were almost unanimous in favor of election of the Senate by the legislatures. The Convention as a whole seemed to feel that, though neither the legislatures nor the people could be trusted alone, election by each of one house of Congress would be the best check against "bad laws."

In the meantime, various minor points had been discussed, and a few of them settled. Randolph's proposals to make congressmen ineligible for a second term, and subject to recall by the voters, had both been dropped, without a word being said in their favor. Madison had sug-

43

gested that, in order to keep national salaries
from fluctuating with the value of money, they
should be paid in wheat.

Franklin had opposed giving the president
any salary, for fear that "the love of power and
the love of money," when coupled with the
"natural inclination in mankind to kingly government," would result sooner or later in turning the president into a king. Whereupon Madison jotted down that the idea "was treated with
great respect, but rather for the author of it,
than from any apparent conviction of its expe-
diency or practicability."

There had been considerable argument over
the length of congressmen's terms. Jennifer of
Maryland wanted them to last three years, so
that the people would not get too bored with voting and neglect to go to the polls. Hamilton
agreed that the terms should last at least three
years, and pointed to the seven-year terms in the
British House of Commons.

But Gerry had insisted that "the people of
New England will never give up the point of an-
nual elections." And Wilson and Randolph also
thought that frequent elections would be more
"familiar and pleasing to the people."

Then Madison had reminded the Convention
—for it was 1787—that "one year will be almost

44

consumed in preparing for and travelling to and from the seat of national business;" and that "the representatives will have to travel seven or eight hundred miles from the distant parts of the union, and will probably not be allowed even a reimbursement of their expenses." Moreover, he had added, they would have to go back home every year to campaign for re-election. So the Convention had compromised on a two-year term.

But behind this easy compromise on minor points, behind the general mistrust of too much democracy—behind all this, and, as in the debate over Senate elections, breaking occasionally within earshot, was the rumble of the approaching storm.

III

"NEVER ON THIS PLAN — NEVER ON ANY OTHER"

THE storm-clouds began to gather early. While the members were still mulling over Randolph's plan at first-hand, before they had turned themselves back from a committee into a convention, the first clash came. They knew all the time that it was coming.

They had decided that the House was to be elected by the people. They had decided that the Senate was to be elected by the state legislatures. Each was then to act as a sort of brake on the other. So far, so good.

But how many men were to be in the House? How many were to be in the Senate? And above all, by what rule were the states to be represented? These were the questions growing in the backs of the members' minds.

The men from the big states wanted proportional representation in the new Congress. If Virginia's population was forty times that of Delaware, they wanted Virginia to have forty members and forty votes in the Senate to Delaware's one, and, if necessary, eighty members and eighty votes in the House to Delaware's two. This was why Madison of Virginia and Wilson of Pennsylvania, both eager for a small Senate, had opposed election of the Senate by the legislatures. Under proportional representation, the smallest states might not be entitled to so much as a single senator.

But the big states started with a handicap, and knew it. In the Congress of the Confederation, the Congress that still existed, there was no such thing as proportional representation. The states were equal, and Delaware's one vote was worth as much as Virginia's.

So in the Convention itself, meeting under the Confederation, the same rule held good. Each state, no matter what its size, no matter how many delegates it had sent, voted as a unit on every question. And if, as often happened, the delegates from any state split evenly in their voting, that state's vote was put down as "divided." In any case, Delaware's vote in the Convention was just as good as Virginia's. And whenever Virginia's vote was divided, Delaware's was worth more.

The men from the small states were of course anxious to hang on to this advantage in the government they were founding. But it was not any vague idea about state rights and state pride that made them anxious. It was fear of what a national government, run by the big states, might do to the industries, the business, even the terri-

50

tory of the small ones.

These men knew that the new government would be given the power to tax. If the big states could always outvote the small, might not national taxes be laid on the goods produced or imported especially by the small states? Might not Virginia's tobacco go tax-free while Rhode Island's rum—or else the sugar and molasses imported to distill it—bore a heavy burden?

The new government would build tariff walls and make commercial treaties with foreign nations. With proportional representation in Congress, might not the tariffs and the treaties favor the industries of the larger states at the expense of the smaller?

The new government would name ports along the Atlantic coast. It would spend money to develop the frontier to the West. Might not the ports be located so as to draw trade to the big states? Might not federal funds be drained to clear their Western frontiers? Might not the small states even be voted out of existence and handed over whole to the big ones?

On the other side, the men from the big states were moved by similar fears to oppose state equality. What they feared was discrimination against their industries and their citizens under a government dominated by the small states.

They could picture the small states getting all the national gravy while the big ones paid the bills. The storm was on its way.

With the Convention still sitting as a committee, Brearley of New Jersey took the floor to make the first move. Quietly, he reminded the delegates that under the Confederation the states voted equally. With the tact of a good politician, he played for the support of the medium-sized states. Under proportional representation, he claimed, "Virginia would have sixteen votes and Georgia but one." This was an exaggeration. "There will be three large states and ten small ones," he said, "and the large states— Massachusetts, Pennsylvania, and Virginia— will carry everything before them."

Paterson, also from New Jersey, was more forceful about it. He questioned the power of the Convention to change the voting rule. We were sent here, he said, only to revise the Confederation, and "we ought to keep within its limits."

Referring back to Randolph's idea that state wealth should count in fixing representation, Paterson asked why a rich state should have more votes in Congress than a poor one, any more than a rich man should have more votes than a poor man. As for proportional representation, he exclaimed, "New Jersey will never confederate on the plan before the committee. She would be swallowed up. I had rather submit to a monarch, to a despot, than to such a fate."

Wilson of Pennsylvania jumped to his feet to reply that "if the small states will not confederate on this plan, Pennsylvania and I presume some other states, will not confederate on any other." "Are not the citizens of Pennsylvania equal to those of New Jersey?" he asked. "Does it require a hundred and fifty of the former to balance fifty of the latter?" Already there seemed to be a complete deadlock.

At this point, Sherman of Connecticut mildly suggested the compromise that was to be adopted weeks later—proportional representation in the House and equal state votes in the Senate. But now his motion was not even seconded. Both sides were still out for all they could get. Each side wanted its scheme of representation in both houses of Congress.

For a short time, a few members held out for other ideas. Rutledge, Butler and Dickinson liked Randolph's plan to make state wealth the important factor, because, as Butler said, "money is power." Franklin outlined a complicated scheme whereby the states, instead of

53

being taxed, would give as much money as they felt like giving to the national government, and would then be represented according to the size of their gifts. It was even suggested that the state lines be erased and then redrawn to make thirteen states of equal size.

But before long the discussion swung back to the main issue. Both sides were eager for a preliminary vote, to show which way the wind was blowing. They knew of course that the vote in committee was not necessarily final.

The first roll-call was on the question of proportional representation in the House. The ayes were overwhelming. Only New Jersey and Delaware held out for state equality. The other small states, suddenly realizing that they could not win everything, had decided on the spur of the moment to save their ammunition for the Senate vote.

Scarcely a minute later, they saw that their strategy had been bad. Georgia and the two Carolinas—encouraged by their fast growth to think they would soon rank with the largest states, hoping their slaves would be counted in their population—sided with Virginia, Pennsylvania and Massachusetts. Equal representation for all states in the Senate was voted down, by six states to five.

It is interesting to see the solid South voting, in 1787, against states' rights. It is also interesting to see New York, at this early date, voting with the smaller states. And the vote itself would have told a different story if the delegates from New Hampshire had not still been delayed in reaching Philadelphia, and if Rhode Island had not refused to send down any delegates at all.

The men from the large states realized this. Hastily they called a vote—and again it was six to five—for proportional representation in the Senate. Hastily they steered the committee into other business. But they well knew that as soon as the committee made its report, favoring proportional representation in both houses of Congress, they would have a fight on their hands.

The fight came sooner than they expected. For a few days, the smaller states seemed to be taking their defeat in silence. But away from the Convention, the delegates from Connecticut, New York, New Jersey, and Delaware were quietly drawing up a plan of their own.

In the meantime, the members, as a committee, had finished revising Randolph's plan and were ready to report it to themselves, as a convention. Suddenly Paterson of New Jersey announced that the small states had drafted an entirely different plan for the new government,

55

and wanted it substituted for the Randolph
plan. So the members, instead of switching back
into a convention, proceeded, still as a committee, to consider the Paterson plan.

As soon as it was read, it became apparent
that the Paterson plan did not really set up a
new government at all. The smaller states,
beaten in their first fight for equal representation
in the Senate, had welched on their earlier will-
ingness to forget the orders that sent them to
Philadelphia. The Paterson plan kept well
within those orders. All it did was revise the
Articles of Confederation.

Congress was to remain the same as under the
Confederation—a single house instead of two,
with members appointed by the states. And in
that Congress, of course, each state was to have
one vote.

It is true that the plan purported to set up a
federal executive and federal courts. But the
federal executive could not enforce laws; he
could only beg the state governors to please enforce them for him. And the federal courts
could only hear federal cases after the state
courts had heard them first. So that actually,
if a state court did not like a federal law, it had
only to acquit everyone charged with violating
that law, and, because a man can not be tried

twice for the same offense, the federal courts would be helpless.

In short, the Paterson plan left the federal government exactly where it was—at the complete mercy of the states. Only in one particular did it seem to increase the federal powers. It gave Congress the right to levy taxes to pay off federal bonds, to raise tariffs for the protection of industry, and to regulate commerce and trade.

Of course, any laws passed to do these things would still have to be enforced by the states. And the states might not want to enforce them. But at least, even in the midst of their biggest battle, both sides of the split Convention still agreed that the central government should be given the power to pay back the money it had borrowed and to protect business and industry. On these points there was no dispute.

Once the Paterson plan was presented, men from the small states arose to defend it. Righteously they reminded the other delegates, though they had neglected to mention it before, that the states had sent them together only to make a few changes in the Confederation. Lansing of New York suddenly thought it "unnecessary and improper to go farther," and spoke of the "want of power in the Convention." "New York," he added, "would never have concurred in sending

57

deputies to the Convention, if she had supposed the deliberations were to turn on a consolidation of the states, and a national government."

Paterson himself took up the thread: "If the confederacy is radically wrong, let us return to our states and obtain larger powers, not assume them ourselves." But a moment later his real reason gave him away. "If a proportional representation be right," he asked, "why do we not vote so here? . . . We have no power to vary the idea of equal sovereignty."

Wilson of Pennsylvania got up to reply: "Will a citizen of Delaware be degraded by becoming a citizen of the United States?" And Randolph, for Virginia, agreed that he was "not scrupulous on the point of power." The Congress of the Confederation, he said, is "a mere diplomatic body." We must have a real national government and "the present is the last moment for establishing one."

But it was Pinckney of South Carolina who hit the nail on the head, so far as the powers of the Convention were concerned. "Give New Jersey an equal vote," he said, "and she will dismiss her scruples."

Now Alexander Hamilton took the floor to make what is often referred to as his "great speech." Although from New York, Hamil-

ton's ideas were miles apart from those of the
two other New York delegates. He knew this,
and later when Yates and Lansing left the
Convention in disgust, he declined to take on
himself alone the responsibility of voting for
New York. So for the last two months of the
Convention, although Hamilton was often
present, New York's vote was never recorded.

Hamilton had been one of the leading figures
in having the Convention called together. Being a well-to-do lawyer in the thick of business
affairs, he resented the haphazard state rule
under the Confederation. He was strong for a
firm national government that would keep the
states and their wild legislatures under its thumb.
Now he outlined to the Convention the kind of
government he wanted to see established.

He did not, he said, like either the Paterson
or the Randolph plan. To stop with the few
small changes of the Paterson plan because of
doubts about the power of the Convention to
go farther "would be to sacrifice the means to
the end." Even the Randolph plan did not go
far enough.

What he wanted was something modelled
after the British government, which he thought,
frankly, was "the best in the world." He went
so far as to admit that he did "not think favor-

ably of republican government." But since he
realized a republican government was going to
be established, he wanted it as close to the British model as possible.

"Their House of Lords," he said, "is a most
noble institution." The American Senate should
be copied from it. Let its members be elected,
but let them be elected by the landed gentry. And
once elected, "let them hold their places for life."

For an executive, he liked the idea of a king.
"The English model," he said, "is the only good
one on this subject." "Let the executive also be
for life." And even though the president be
elected, let it again be written in the Constitution that the poor shall have no vote in electing
him.

What, then, was to happen to the states?
What rights would they keep under a modified
copy of the British government? Hamilton
wanted no half-way measures. "As states," he
said, "they ought to be abolished." He did not
object to their being turned into departments
or minor divisions of the nation. But he insisted that, if this were done, their governors
be appointed by the national government, and
given the absolute power to veto all state laws.
This was to be his safe-guard against paper-
money measures. This was his answer to the

Paterson plan.

Now, Madison too, devoted his main speech of the Convention to chiding the small states for their sudden squeamishness about scrapping the Confederation. Not so extreme as Hamilton in his ideas, he nevertheless agreed heartily that a strong national government must be established, and that it must be established now or never.

He explained the difference between a national, and a federal government, such as the small states wanted to keep. A national government, drawing its power from the people, would be absolutely supreme. But in a federal government, drawing its power from the states themselves, the states would still hold the upper hand.

And why prefer a national government? Because of the abundant evidence of what happens under a federal one. Because of "the emissions of paper money and other kindred measures." Because "the creditor states must suffer unjustly from every emission by the debtor states."

Could not evils of this sort be stopped by federal laws? Again the evidence was answer. "The violations of the federal articles," said Madison, "have been numerous and notorious." And, he added, with a quick glance toward Pat-

61

erson, "among the most notorious was an act of New Jersey herself."

For other reasons, too, a national government was necessary. The states had been ignoring the Confederation's treaties with foreign countries. Further violations might even lead to war. The central government must be able to enforce such treaties, and avert this "greatest of national calamities."

Moreover, Madison continued,—a touch of sarcasm in his words—if the small states really are afraid of being destroyed by the large ones, have they not a great deal more to fear while they remain virtually separate nations? "Will the small states be more secure against the ambition and power of their larger neighbors than they would be under a general government?"

Then, growing more persuasive, Madison told the small states to "consider the expence of maintaining their delegates in Congress." Under a national government, he implied, they would not have to pay these bills. And in case the point seemed silly, he reminded the Convention that, for a time, Delaware's sole spokesman in the Confederation Congress had been a citizen, and a state official at that, of Pennsylvania.

With a final plea to the small states, Madison asked them to look to the future when there might be other states even smaller than they. "The prospect of many new states to the westward is another consideration of importance." And the smaller states of the original thirteen would in turn want to outvote these Western states, coming into the union "when they contain but few inhabitants." "Let them have an equal vote," he concluded, "and a more objectionable minority than ever might give law to the whole."

This was clever argument and, at least so far as New York was concerned, good prophecy at the same time. But two of the three New York delegates were not looking so far ahead. Instead, it was Connecticut which was swung over, along with part of the Maryland delegation, by the force of Madison's eloquence.

Hardly had Madison taken his seat than a vote was called for the committee to choose between Paterson's plan and Randolph's, as revised. With New Hampshire still absent and with Maryland divided, the count was seven to three. Only New Jersey, New York, and Delaware still held out for a federal, instead of a national, government.

Immediately, and at long last, the members turned themselves back from a committee into a convention. And as a convention, they began to go over again, point by point, the revised Ran-

63

dolph plan. That plan, as reported and recommended, called for proportional representation in both houses of Congress. In their first big battle, the smaller states had gone down to complete defeat.

IV

FROM HARMONY BACK TO DISCORD

THE smaller states did not take defeat any too graciously. They knew of course that their biggest fight was still ahead of them, when the Convention, as a convention, was to take up again the question of representation in Congress. Even so, there was grumbling and grousing as the members started to go over, and round out, the revised Randolph plan.

There was objection to the use of the word "national." The states having been equal under a federal government, Martin of Maryland "could never accede to a plan that would introduce an inequality and lay ten states at the mercy of Virginia, Massachusetts, and Pennsylvania."

Lansing of New York brought up a new point, which has a familiar ring today. He thought the whole business too radical—a dangerous experiment. It was "too novel and complex," he said. "No man can foresee what its operation will be."

Then Mason of Virginia made the interesting reply that "the Convention, though comprising so many distinguished characters, can not be expected to make a faultless government." He, for one, "would prefer trusting to posterity the amendment of its defects."

Wilson of Pennsylvania introduced a patriotic note by reading the Declaration of Independence. And the big states, flushed by their recent victory, agreed unanimously to leave out the word "national," realizing that this gesture did not make a particle of difference in the plan.

There was objection to setting up two houses of Congress, in place of the single house under the Confederation. Sherman of Connecticut— perhaps regretting already Connecticut's vote for the Randolph plan the day before—reminded the delegates that the existing Congress "carried us through the War." He admitted that, "money matters being the most important of all," Congress must somehow be given the power to get money to pay back the federal loans. But he still insisted that, if Congress was going to have two branches, the states must be given an equal vote in at least one of them.

Johnson of Connecticut wanted to know whether the states would retain any rights at all under this new-fangled national government. But Wilson replied that he did not particularly see why they should. He thought that the real trouble was "that in spite of every precaution, the general government will be in perpetual danger of encroachments from the state governments."

Then Madison, who made a habit of speaking just before a vote was taken, got up to inquire why all this quibbling about state rights. "Why," he asked, "should it follow that the general government would take from the states any branch of their power as far as its operation is beneficial?" Townships, for instance, do not complain when the states take on jobs that the states can handle better. And surely, "the people will not be less free as members of one great republic than as members of thirteen small ones."

Getting down to brass tacks, he reminded the Convention of the "gloomy consequences" of leaving the state governments with the upper hand. Merely imagining what the states would do, with more of their paper money laws and their impediments to business and trade, "must have formed the chief motive with those present to undertake the arduous task" of founding a strong national government.

Again, Madison, with this pointed plea, had convinced the Connecticut delegates. On the vote for a new Congress, with two separate branches, New York, New Jersey, and Delaware remained the only dissenters.

For three or four days now, there was pretty

general agreement. Both large and small states voted to leave unchanged the election of the House by the people, and of the Senate by the state legislatures. Much of the time was spent in going over small details, and on the surface everything seemed calm. Actually, it was only a break in the storm.

Whether Congress should be paid by the states, or by the national government, caused some discussion. Ellsworth thought the different standards of living in the states would make a regular national salary unfair. Williamson agreed that the states ought to pay their own representatives, especially because of "the prospect of new states to the Westward." They would be poor and they would have strange ideas when they came into the union, and he did not see why the old states should "pay the expences of men who will be employed in thwarting their measures and interests."

But Madison, fearing that payment by the states would put Congress under state control, replied that any new Western states "ought to be considered as equals and brethren." He disliked particularly, he said, "the policy suggested by Mr. Williamson of leaving the members from the poor states beyond the mountains to the precarious and parsimonious support of their constituents."

As for the Senate, Pinckney and Franklin thought that senators should get no salary at all. They were "to represent the wealth of the country," and should be rich enough in their own right. Morris agreed: "The Senate must have great personal property; it must have the aristocratic spirit; it must love to lord it through pride." And Mason added that, since the purpose of the Senate was "to secure the rights of property," only well-to-do men should be eligible to membership.

But over Hamilton's objection that "those who pay are the masters of those who are paid," and Randolph's that "we are going too far in consulting popular prejudices," it was voted that salaries, for both senators and congressmen, be paid by the states that sent them. And it was not until almost two months later that this provision was changed. Then, Dickinson urged "the necessity of making the general government independent of the prejudices, passions, and improper views of the state legislatures," and it was agreed almost unanimously that the salaries come out of the national treasury.

The minimum age for senators had been set, in the committee, at thirty years. No age had been named for congressmen, though it had of

71

course been taken for granted they must be twenty-one. Now, Mason moved to bar all those under twenty-five. He spoke of "the deficiency of young politicians," and called it "absurd that a man today should not be permitted by the law to make a bargain for himself, and tomorrow should be authorized to manage the affairs of a great nation."

Mason himself was sixty years old. Wilson, politely failing to mention this fact, answered that he saw "no more reason for incapacitating youth than age." But in spite of Wilson's warning that "the motion tends to damp the efforts of genius and of laudable ambition," it was carried easily. The delegates, though comparatively young themselves, seemed to feel that their affairs and those of the nation would not be so safe in the hands of men even younger than they.

This same undertone of conservatism welled up even more strongly over the length of senators' terms. Though still bitterly at odds as to whether the large or the small states should control the Senate, the members agreed wholeheartedly that, no matter who controlled it, it should be a bulwark of protection against the democratic House.

The House was to be elected every two years,

and might be swayed by wild, popular ideas. The Senate must stand firmly against such ideas. When Randolph said "wisdom and stability" demanded that no more than a third of the Senate go out of office at any election, not a voice was raised against him.

Now, Madison, speaking for a long Senate term, put into a nut-shell his theory of government. Madison is known, today, as "the father of the Constitution." He was among the most active in calling the Convention together and, later, in getting the finished Constitution ratified. There is no doubt that he had a large hand in drafting the Randolph plan from which the Constitution grew. And in the Convention, it was he who spoke most often—and most effectively. For he spoke, at bottom, the sentiments of his fellow-members. In Madison's beliefs, as he now put them into measured words, lay the philosophy back of the Constitution.

The new government, he implied, was not actually to be run by the people; they were not to be their own rulers. Instead, the government was "to protect the people against their rulers." But the government, although it was to protect the people, must also be protected against them.

The people, said Madison, are subject to

73

"transient impressions" and "temporary errors," and "are liable to err from fickleness and passion." "A necessary fence against this danger will be to select a portion of enlightened citizens, whose limited number and firmness may seasonably interpose against impetuous councils."

✗ In plain language, what was this danger against which the Senate must stand guard? Madison explained—nor did he mince his words. "In all civilized countries," he said, "the people fall into different classes having a real or supposed difference of interests. There will be creditors and debtors, farmers, merchants and manufacturers. There will be particularly the distinction of rich and poor."

"An increase in population," he went on, "will of necessity increase the proportion of those who will labour under all the hardships of life, and secretly sigh for a more equal distribution of its blessings. These may in time outnumber those who are placed above the feeling of indigence. According to the equal laws of suffrage, the power will slide into the hands of the former."

As soon, then, as the poor could outvote the rich, they would make plans for a more equal distribution of wealth. And the Senate, to make sure it would vote down these "symptoms of a levelling spirit," must be a highly "respectable"

74

body. A long term for senators would help, Madison concluded,—help to protect the rich against the "injustice" of popular laws, of the sort we know all too sadly from "our own experience."

Certainly, there was good prophecy behind Madison's reasoning. There was also a frank and pointed statement that the Convention had gathered to set up a government along lines that could scarcely be labelled democratic.

No word of protest came from the other delegates.

Madison favored a nine-year Senate term, but even those who talked for a shorter term agreed that "stability" and "respectability" were essential. Several of the members liked Hamilton's idea of having senators elected for life. And in the end, when the term was set at six years, it was mainly for strategic reasons. As Gerry said: "A longer term would defeat itself. It never would be adopted by the people."

* * *

From this telling display of agreement about guarding the new government against popular rule, the Convention rushed headlong into its biggest battle. How, for the final time, should the states be represented in the two houses of Congress? The fight was on.

75

Martin of Maryland fired the opening gun. It turned out to be a siege. For over three hours, Martin harangued the delegates about the horrors of proportional representation. He warned against "dissolution of the states;" he questioned again the powers of the Convention; he expressed the usual fears that the three big states would become "compleat masters of the rest"; and at the end, he said he was "too much exhausted to finish his remarks," and would have to continue tomorrow. The members promptly adjourned.

Next day, Martin was up again. Madison grew tired of reporting his speech, and jotted down that it was "delivered with much diffuseness and considerable vehemence." But the small states were in sympathy. Lansing of New York and Dayton of New Jersey rose immediately to endorse everything Martin had said.

Williamson of North Carolina finally got the floor to remind the small states again of the commercial threat of new states to the West. If they should get an equal vote, they would put national taxes on business and on sales "which would fall with greatest weight on the old states." And Madison tried to quiet any fears that the three big states would gang up on the others. They have completely different interests, he said, "the staple of Massachusetts being fish, of Pennsylvania flour, of Virginia tobacco."

But Sherman of Connecticut could not see why a big state should have more votes than a small one. "The rich man who enters into society along with the poor man gives up more than the poor man, yet with an equal vote he is equally safe." At least, this was the theory on which the states were equal under the Confederation.

Benjamin Franklin was getting worried by all the bickering. "The small progress we have made after four or five weeks," he said, "is methinks a melancholy proof of the imperfection of human understanding." It would be appropriate now to turn, as a last resort, to God, for "without his concurring aid we shall succeed in this political building no better than the builders of Babel." He suggested daily prayers, and "that one or more of the clergy of this city be requested to officiate in that service."

Hamilton, always practical, objected. He did not want the news to leak out that the Convention was having trouble. The other members agreed that secrecy was more important than divine assistance. Out of respect for Franklin, they took no vote, but instead adjourned for the day. The battle continued, without benefit of prayer.

Little attention was paid when Johnson of Connecticut recommended the compromise that his fellow-statesman, Sherman, had suggested earlier — proportional representation in the House and equal votes in the Senate. "The controversy must be endless," he said, "whilst gentlemen differ." But the controversy went on.

Gorham of Massachusetts pointed out that the big states would soon be split up anyway. Maine was going to break off from Massachusetts, and Virginia would lose Kentucky. And Madison —again the wise prophet—warned that leaving the states with too much control of national affairs would lead to civil war. "The same causes which have rendered the old world the theatre of incessant wars, and have banished liberty from the face of it, would soon produce the same effects here."

Hamilton, realizing that the Convention he had helped call together was fast getting nowhere, admitted "it is a miracle we are now here," and thought "it would be madness to trust to future miracles." A strong national government must be established now, or it never will be. "We should run every risk," he added, "in trusting to future amendments."

Madison, however, was against taking chances

78

of this kind. A strong national government should be established, all right, but it must have control right from the start; for "leaving future amendments to posterity is a dangerous doctrine." Not that amendments may not well be needed in later years. But because "the fear of innovation, the hue and cry in favor of the liberty of the people, will prevent the necessary reform."

Gerry of Massachusetts, also anxious to squelch state rights, accused the small states of being "intoxicated with the idea of their sovereignty." Of course, he, like the other delegates from the big states, was satisfied with the plan then existing, for proportional representation in both houses of Congress. He therefore lamented "that instead of coming here like a band of brothers, belonging to the same family, we seem to have brought with us the spirit of political negotiators."

Now it was time for the first vote. The question was whether the states should be equal in the House of Representatives. The answer was no. But it was not so strong a no as had been registered in the committee. Six states carried the day, with Maryland divided, where nine had voted for proportional representation before. The small states were not being fooled into bad

79

strategy a second time.

The Senate question came next. The small states began to get panicky. Desperately, they asked that a hurry call be sent out for the New Hampshire delegates, and that the Convention be adjourned until they arrive.

The reply of the large states was brief and sarcastic. "They are not unapprized of the meeting," snapped Rutledge, "and can attend if they choose. Rhode Island might as well be urged to appoint and send deputies."

The fight grew hotter, and the speeches more oratorical. Wilson of Pennsylvania claimed to defend "the inherent, indisputable and unalienable rights of men." Is the new government, he asked, "to be for men, or for the imaginary beings called states?" If the small states, he threatened, refuse to join the large "on just and proper principles, if a separation must take place, it could never happen on better grounds."

Ellsworth shot back that Connecticut, at least, was being impartial—which was more than could be said for the big states. Connecticut's population was neither large nor small. It was half way between. Yet Connecticut could not see that any "just and proper principles" required that the large states be given more votes than the small ones.

"We are razing the foundations of the building," charged Ellsworth, "when we need only repair the roof." And with a final taunting reminder of the Confederation rule, he hoped "that some regard will still be paid to the plighted faith under which each state holds an equal right of suffrage in the general councils."

Speaking of "plighted faith," retorted Madison, he for one thought "that the party claiming from others an adherence to a common engagement ought at least to be guiltless itself of a violation. Of all the states, however, Connecticut is perhaps least able to urge this plea." It was Connecticut that "by a pretty recent vote, positively refused to pass a law for complying with the requisitions of Congress."

Ellsworth jumped to his feet again to boast of Connecticut's record in the Revolutionary War. "The muster rolls will show she had more troops in the field than Virginia." The fight was narrowing down to personalities.

King of Massachusetts tried another tack. He predicted that "a government founded in a vicious principle of representation must be as short lived as it would be unjust." Dayton of New Jersey immediately replied: "When assertion is given for proof and terror substituted for argument, I presume they will have no effect

81

however eloquently spoken."

Now, Bedford of Delaware threw a bomb into the proceedings. He began by accusing the big states of being "dictated by interest, by ambition." "Are not," he demanded, "the large states evidently seeking to aggrandize themselves at the expense of the small?"

"We have been told with a dictatorial air that this is the last moment for a fair trial in favor of a good government." Bedford was growing more heated. As a matter of fact, he shouted, "the large states dare not dissolve the Confederation. If they do, the small ones will find some foreign ally of more honor and good faith, who will take them by the hand and do them justice."

The members were genuinely shocked. Randolph deplored "the warm and rash language of Mr. Bedford." And King, a bit piously, was "grieved that such a thought had entered into his heart and more grieved that such an expression had dropped from his lips. The gentleman can only excuse it to himself on the score of passion."

But soon it was Bedford's turn to cry: for shame! Gouverneur Morris of Pennsylvania blurted out: "This country must be united. If persuasion does not unite it, the sword will."

And Bedford, quick to his feet, apologized for his own outburst, and demanded a similar apology from Morris.

It came time for the all-important vote on representation in the Senate. The New Hampshire delegates had not yet arrived. The small states, beaten before by one vote in the committee, rallied their forces and held their thumbs.

All the way down the line, the states voted as they had before. The roll-call went from North to South. It was five to five when it reached Georgia, last on the list. And Georgia, —half of its delegates perhaps made cautious by the vehemence of the three big states, in the debate that was just over—reported its vote as divided. The score, this time, was a tie.

"We are now at a full stop," was Sherman's comment. And Williamson added: "If we do not concede on both sides, our business must soon be at an end."

V

THE MELODY LINGERS ON

CONCESSION looked impossible on the floor of the Convention. The delegates on both sides had been worked up to a fever pitch by the warmth of their own and their opponents' arguments. Perhaps a smaller group might be able to talk things over in a more friendly way.

With this thought in mind, a committee was suggested, to help iron out the difficulty. Madison objected that it would be a waste of time because, as soon as the committee had reported, the fight would only start all over again. He realized there was nothing the big states could concede, short of equal votes in the Senate for the small states.

Nevertheless, a committee was elected. It was made up of one man from each state. Divided Georgia was represented by Abraham Baldwin, who had just sided with his state of birth, Connecticut, for equality of all states in the Senate.

While the rest of the delegates adjourned to celebrate the Fourth of July, the committee went to work. And it was Benjamin Franklin who, after long but peaceful discussion, proposed the compromise which the committee quickly accepted. The smaller states were to get their equal votes in the Senate. In return, the House, which would presumably be controlled by the large states, was to have the sole right to originate money bills. And these money bills could not then be changed by the Senate in any way, but only passed or rejected.

This compromise, though it was later modified, was the turning point of the Convention. In itself, it indicated the real basis of the fight between the large and small states. That fight was not over the purpose of the Convention, nor was it founded on a gallant defense of state rights against national power. It sprang from the fear, common to both groups, that a national government controlled by the other would discriminate unfairly in matters pertaining to money. And on that score, the compromise seemed to offer a safe-guard to both.

But the fight was not yet ended. No sooner was the proposed compromise read to the Convention than Madison repeated, a little testily, that he would brook no compromise at all with the "just principles" of proportional representation. Moreover—and more significantly—he said that he could "not regard the privilege of originating money bills as any concession on the side of the small states."

Wilson explained why there was "nothing like a concession here." If the Senate could so much as reject money bills, it could keep on rejecting them until it got the kind of bill it wanted. "If both branches are to say yes or no, it is of little consequence which should say yes or no first."

And Gouverneur Morris accused the small states of taking unfair advantage of the Confederation rule. When the Confederation was formed, he said, "the small states, aware of the necessity of preventing anarchy, and taking advantage of the moment, extorted from the large ones an equality of votes." Did the small states honestly think that preservation of their suddenly precious rights, as states, would result in an efficient form of government? "Good God, Sir, is it possible they can so delude themselves?"

Thus a few delegates from the large states clung for a while, with lingering stubbornness, to their wish to control completely the new government. Their apparent refusal to give so much as an inch angered and disgusted Yates and Lansing. These two packed their bags, left Philadelphia, and did not return.

Hamilton, the other New York delegate, had gone home earlier to attend to business. He did

89

not stay away permanently but, for several days now, only ten states were represented at the Convention. Fear grew that other men might follow in the steps of Yates and Lansing. Yet, as Sherman said, it was "the wish of everyone that some general government should be established." Above all, the Convention must not be allowed to break up in failure.

Gerry of Massachusetts reminded his brethren from the larger states that "something must be done." Else, "what is to become of our treaties, what of our foreign debts, what of our domestic?" And Mason, who had represented Virginia on the committee, joined in chiding those who would accept no compromise. As for him: "I would bury my bones in this city rather than expose my country to the consequences of a dissolution of the Convention without anything being done."

Mason's challenge worked like magic. There was no more quibbling as to whether giving the House full control of money bills was enough of a concession to the big states. The Convention went on to consider other points brought up by the compromise plan.

And weeks later, after the money bills provision had been written into the first draft of the Constitution, it was Mason who still de-

90

fended it most strongly. "If the Senate can originate," he predicted, "they will in the recess of the legislative sessions, hatch their mischievous projects, for their own purposes, and have their money bills ready cut and dried (to use a common phrase) for the meeting of the House of Representatives."

But by that time, the fight between large and small states had been pretty well forgotten. The large states themselves no longer wanted the crust that had been tossed them in return for equal state votes in the Senate. Remembering that the House, although they would control it, was really to represent the people, against whose notions the Senate was to stand guard, they joined with the small states in throwing out entirely the provision that money bills should come from the House alone. And when reference was made to the compromise in an effort to have the provision put back, Madison asked indignantly, since most of the big states no longer wanted it, "what obligation can the small states be under to concur against their judgments in reinstating the section?"

And it was still later, after Dickinson had pointed out that disputes between House and Senate "could not be avoided any way" that the provision was finally agreed to, in greatly modi-

91

fied form. As modified, it gave the House alone
the right to originate, not all money bills, but
those "for raising revenue." And it gave the
Senate, as a check against popular laws, the
right, not only to reject these bills, but also to
alter or amend them.

But all this was yet to come. Meanwhile, on
the floor of the Convention, the delegates were
still hashing over the question of representation
in Congress. The compromise plan had not yet
been put to a vote.

There was no more talk of proportional representation in the Senate. The large states now
realized that if they pressed this point further,
they might find themselves with no Constitution
at all. But they were still unwilling to give
the small states equal votes, if they could put
across some other method of representation.

The notion was suggested of dividing the
states, according to size, into three classes, and
giving them one, two, or three senators respectively. The plan never got very far. Although
half-way between proportional representation
and equal votes, it seemed too artificial and
arbitrary.

Suddenly the big states began to argue for
Senate representation according to state wealth.
Here was a scheme that might appeal to the small

states, in view of the general agreement on the purpose of the Senate. It had been part of the original Randolph plan but had been lost by the wayside in the course of the battle.

Baldwin of Georgia resurrected it. He took for granted that the Senate "ought to be the representation of property," and urged that "in forming it therefore some reference ought to be had to the relative wealth of its constituents." Gerry of Massachusetts also spoke in favor of a "combined ratio of numbers of inhabitants and of wealth," and his fellow-statesman, King, stood up to agree with him.

All along the line, the men from the big states took up the cry. Butler of South Carolina "contended strenuously," as Madison put it, "that property was the only just measure of representation." Davie of North Carolina chimed in that "wealth or property ought to be represented in the second branch." Gorham of Massachusetts, Pinckney of South Carolina, Morris of Pennsylvania, and others joined the chorus.

Then Rutledge of South Carolina moved that representation in Congress be "according to the principles of wealth and population." With the motion, it seemed to dawn on the delegates that the principle of wealth was a little vague. Although quite in keeping with their intention that the Senate should be the guardian of property, the rule itself would be too hard to apply.

Even the large states realized this at once. Mason of Virginia and Wilson of Pennsylvania called the idea "too indefinite and impracticable." "Too vague," said Paterson of New Jersey, who did not like the scheme anyway. And Sherman of Connecticut pointed out the catch in it. State wealth would run about the same as state population, and the small states would find themselves with proportional representation in the Senate too.

The scheme was dropped, but not because of any objection to a government in which wealth would be represented. As Johnson of Connecticut put it, "wealth and population are the true, equitable rule of representation; but these two principles resolve themselves into one, population being the best measure of wealth." And, whatever else the small states wanted, they did not want the large states to control both House and Senate.

In the meantime, the question whether one particular kind of wealth should count toward representation in Congress had begun to split the Convention along new lines. The men who had argued hardest for a rule that included wealth came from the states to the South. It grew more and more apparent that the wealth they especially wanted represented was embodied in their negro slaves.

Seventy-odd years before it broke, came the first rumblings of the Civil War. If slaves, as wealth, were not to help swell the number of Southern congressmen, then, insisted the South, the slaves must be counted as people. The slaveless "Eastern" states—as they were then called —immediately objected. Paterson of New Jersey could "regard negro slaves in no light but as property." "Has a man in Virginia," he asked, "a number of votes in proportion to the number of his slaves?"

Undaunted, Butler and Pinckney of South Carolina moved that the full number of slaves in each state be counted in figuring up relative state populations. But most of the Southern delegates did not ask so much. They wanted three-fifths of the slaves to count toward representation in the House.

The three-fifths fraction was not chosen at random. The Confederation Congress, unable itself to collect taxes, had to ask the separate states to supply it with money. And under the Confederation rule, three-fifths of the slaves were counted in dividing up these request taxes,

95

according to population, among the states.

But this was not a question of apportioning taxes, came the reply. It was a question of the representation of citizens in Congress. "Are the blacks admitted as citizens?" demanded Wilson of Pennsylvania. "Then why are they not admitted on an equality with white citizens? Are they admitted as property? Then why is not other property admitted into the computation?"

Morris of Pennsylvania was more indignant. He could never, he exclaimed, "agree to give such encouragement to the slave trade as would be given by allowing the Southern states a representation for their negroes." And on the first vote as to whether three-fifths of the slaves should be counted, the South was defeated by six states to four.

It was the turn of the slave states to threaten to leave the Convention. A similar threat seemed to have worked wonders for the small states' interests. So Davie of North Carolina felt it was "high time now to speak out." He was sure "that North Carolina will never confederate on any terms that do not rate the blacks at least as three-fifths. If the Eastern states mean, therefore, to exclude them altogether, the business is at an end."

96

Randolph was not so violent, in voicing Virginia's views. Although "lamenting that such a species of property exists," he felt that since it did exist, the slave states needed the "security" of extra votes in Congress. His implication was clear. He was afraid, as were all of the Southern delegates, that if the Eastern states controlled Congress they might vote to abolish slavery altogether.

But Gouverneur Morris, still strong against slavery, had another idea about security. If the South should be granted representation for its slaves, the South might control Congress. And "if the Southern states get the power into their hands, and be joined as they will be with the interior country, they will inevitably bring on a war with Spain for the Mississippi."

Butler of South Carolina was getting sick of the taunts Morris was directing at the slave states. "The security the Southern states want," he shot back, "is that their negroes may not be taken from them, which some gentlemen within or without doors have a very good mind to do."

It was for King of Massachusetts to turn conciliator, before tempers were lost a second time. He had realized all along that the real fight lay "not between the great and small states, but between the Southern and Eastern." Why? Be-

97

cause one of the chief purposes of the new government would be, by regulation, to protect and encourage manufacturing and business. This would be of no help to the plantation states of the South, and might even hurt them by raising the prices they would have to pay for goods made in New England shops and mills. Suppose, on top of this, that slaves should not count toward seats in Congress. Then, as Pinckney had described the position of the slave states, "if they are to form so considerable a minority, and the regulation of trade is to be given to the general government, they will be nothing more than overseers for the Northen states."

Suppose, moreover, there should be any attempt in the future to abolish or restrict slavery. Then, said King, looking well into the next century, "he must be shortsighted indeed who does not foresee that whenever the Southern states shall be more numerous than the Northern, they can and will hold a language that will awe them into justice. If they threaten to separate now in case injury shall be done them, will their threats be less urgent or effectual when force shall back their demands?"

But it was a more practical argument, with a sentimental ring to it, that finally convinced the North. How about taxation? Would not part of the national taxes be collected through the states, as they were under the Confederation? Would not three-fifths of the slaves count in apportioning these taxes between the states, as they did under the Confederation?

Yet if the Southern states were to have no more votes in Congress because of their slaves, would it be fair to make them pay more taxes because of their slaves? King hammered his point home with the battle-cry of the Revolution. "Taxation and representation," he said, quietly, "ought to go together."

The delegates could not know that the new government never would—as it never did—levy a "direct" tax and apportion it among the states. They voted that in figuring state populations, whether to divide up "direct" taxes or to assign seats in the House, three-fifths of the slaves should count as people.

The dragon of North-South dissension did not raise its head again until some time later. But Gouverneur Morris was still bothered by geographical monsters. If the commercial East was not to be protected against the agricultural South, he wanted it protected against the farming states that would spring up to the West.

He opposed the regular taking of a census to vary representation in the House with shifts

99

of population. No matter how far West the frontier should be pushed, the thirteen original states, he felt, should hang on to their control of the national government. He warned of "the danger of throwing a preponderancy into the Western scale, since in time the Western people will outnumber the Atlantic states," and was anxious "therefore to put it in the power of the latter to keep a majority of votes in their own hands."

To Mason's more generous insistence that "the Western states must be treated as equals," Morris retorted: "The remarks of Mr. Mason relative to the Western country have not changed my opinion. Among other objections it must be apparent they will not be able to furnish men equally enlightened to share in the administration of our common interests. The busy haunts of men, not the remote wilderness, are the proper school of political talents."

This was too much for Madison. Morris, he said, was a little inconsistent. After assuring the South it had nothing to fear from a Northern majority in Congress, "he is still more zealous in exhorting all to a jealousy of a Western majority." Apparently, said Madison, "the gentleman determines the human character by the points of the compass."

100

The jibe was effective. Pennsylvania, in the face of Morris' opposition, joined in voting for a census, to be taken every ten years.

It was now settled that representation in the House should be according to state population. It was settled that the Southern states could count three-fifths of their slaves. It was settled that population should be determined regularly by a government census. But whether, in line with the committee's compromise, all states, large and small, should be equal in the Senate had not yet been put to a final vote.

The large states made one more desperate effort to stave off the inevitable. King of Massachusetts, evading the real point, still could not see what "state rights" had to do with the question. "The general government," according to his notion, "can never wish to intrude on the state governments."

Madison, fighting to the last, made King's meaning clear with a suggestion of his own. "In all cases," he proposed, "where the general government is to act on the people, let the people be represented and the votes be proportional. In all cases where the government is to act on the states, let the states be represented and the votes be equal."

"But," challenged Madison, "give me a single

101

instance in which the general government is not to operate on the people individually." This challenge pretty well demolished the small states' pretense that they wanted equality in the Senate in order to protect against national power their rights, as states. It did not, of course, persuade the small states to give up equality in the Senate, and thus open the way to possible discriminations against the commerical interests of their citizens.

Now Gerry of Massachusetts made a clever appeal to those same commercial interests, which the small states were bound to protect at all costs. Taking a leaf from Morris' book, he warned of "dangers apprehended from Western states" if all states should have equal votes in the Senate. He did not like the idea of "putting ourselves in their hands. They will, if they acquire power, like all men, abuse it. They will oppress commerce and drain our wealth into the Western country."

But Sherman of Connecticut refused to be frightened. He pooh-poohed the danger with a bad prediction. "There is no probability," he scoffed, "that the number of future states will exceed that of the existing states." "Besides," he added, a bit more wisely, "we are providing for our posterity, for our children and our grandchildren, who are as likely to be citizens of new Western states as of the old states."

To the contrary, "foreigners are resorting to that country," replied Gerry. But the small states paid no attention.

Martin of Maryland was getting annoyed by these last-ditch tactics. "The states that please to call themselves large," he flung out, "are the weakest in the Union. Look at Massachusetts. Look at Virginia. Are they efficient states?"

Wilson of Pennsylvania was stung into replying: "I suppose the next assertion will be that the small states are richer, also; though I hardly expect it will be persisted in when the states are called on for taxes and troops." For a minute, it seemed that the fire-works were to start all over again.

But before any further outbursts, there was a call for the vote that was to prove decisive. With New York and Rhode Island absent, with New Hampshire not yet on the floor, it looked as though this time, compromise or no compromise, the large states must surely win.

The roll-call started with Massachusetts. And when that champion of the big states reported its vote as divided, the story was as good as told. Gerry and Strong, fearing that defeat for the small states would bring the Convention to an

103

end, had decided to support the compromise plan. As King wrote in his diary, "to my mortification," it was Massachusetts that turned the tide.

Then North Carolina voted for the compromise, rather than risk no Constitution at all, and the battle was over. Only Pennsylvania, Virginia, and South Carolina—and Georgia, voting when its vote no longer mattered—held out to the end. After more than a month of fighting, the small states had finally won the right to be represented equally in the Senate.

Next morning, before the Convention opened, the big states held an indignation meeting. As Madison put it, "the time was wasted in vague conversation." And when, later, Gouverneur Morris moved to reconsider the vote, his motion was not even seconded. "It was probably," noted Madison, "approved by several members who either despaired of success, or were apprehensive that the attempt would inflame the jealousies of the smaller states."

And before the Convention was over, the small states saw to it that they should never, short of revolution, be deprived of their hard-won victory. The Constitution forbids forever just one type of amendment. It is an amendment which would take away from any state,

104

without its consent, its equal vote in the Senate.

Because of the length of the battle between the large and small states, because of the bitterness which occasionally marked it, it is often talked of today as a clash between two groups with fundamentally different theories of government. The large states are pictured as champions of strong national power; the small states as doughty defenders of local self-government as embodied in the notion of state rights. Sometimes the position of the small states is even twisted to make them guardians of the people's liberties against the centralizing tendencies of a 1787 brand of fascism. But the debates tell a different story.

Until the small states lost the first vote for equality in Congress, there was no objection to setting up a strong national government—even in the face of explicit orders to the contrary. There was no objection after the small states had won back equality in the Senate. "Give New Jersey an equal vote and she will dismiss her scruples," was more than an idle jest.

It was because they too favored strong national power—and knew that it would be given to the new government—that the small states fought tooth and nail for equal votes in the Senate. They did not want that power to fall

105

into the hands of the large states. They did not want it used at the expense of their own commercial interests, when it was used to tax and to regulate business and trade.

Only when their business interests differed did the delegates to the Convention violently disagree. The South fought, not for state rights, but for assurance that it would not lose its slaves. The North fought for protection of its manufacturing interests against the fast-growing agricultural sections to the South and the West.

When their interests were identical, the delegates did not waste time over basic principles. Large and small states, North and South, agreed that the new government must curb the state legislatures with their wild, popular laws. That was one of the chief aims that had brought the Convention together. And even in the midst of their bitterest battles, the delegates joined in advocating the protection—not of life, not of liberty, but of property.

King called property "the primary object of society." Morris thought it was "the main object of society," and therefore "the main object of government." Rutledge, as though saying two and two are four, remarked that "property is certainly the principal object of society."

Butler took it as a matter of course that the Convention was founding "a government instituted principally for the protection of property." And Pinckney, too, felt that the Constitution was to be the basis of "a government instituted for the protection of property."

Only Wilson could not, he said, "agree that property is the sole or primary object of government and society. The cultivation and improvement of the human mind is the most noble object." But the very fact that Wilson's was the lone voice raised against the chorus merely emphasized the agreement of the other members.

The fights between the large and small states, and between the North and South, did not disrupt for long the basic harmony of the Convention. Beneath the surface discord, the melody lingered on.

VI

THE STATES ARE PUT IN THEIR PLACES

THE Convention hummed with harmony as soon as the Senate battle had been left behind. Almost casually, and in haphazard order, the delegates went on to round out the rest of the Constitution. Every once in a while a point would come up on which rival groups of interests had differing ideas and differing desires. But discussion was, for the most part, sober and unimpassioned. There was no more talk of picking up toys and going home.

It took only a minute to decide that each state should have two senators. Everyone favored a small Senate as more efficient, and tending toward dignity in its members. But to allow only one senator apiece would be to risk taking all representation away from a state whenever its lone member could not be present. And on the other hand, three or more senators per state would mean "additional expence," as well as making the exclusive group "too numerous."

That each state's two senators, then, should vote separately in their own names, instead of jointly in the name of the state, was no sooner suggested than it was almost unanimously adopted. And this in spite of the fact that

111

Martin described the plan accurately as "departing from the idea of the *states* being represented in the second branch." The small states no longer cared who was represented, so long as the large states would not have control.

The problem of how to elect the president kept bobbing up from time to time. Here, as in the disputes over Congress, the small states were afraid to put the election in the hands of the large states. All through the summer, the question would first be considered, then postponed, then re-considered, then decided, then, a few days later, re-opened all over again. And though no bitterness marked these recurring discussions, it was not until the closing days of the Convention that the delegates settled on the complicated plan that they wrote into the Constitution.

But it took no time at all, and very little discussion, to set up the Supreme Court, the third branch of the new government. Under the original Randolph plan, the judges, like the president, were to be elected by Congress. Some delegates had objected that this would result in "intrigue" and "partiality." They felt the president would do a better job of picking a Supreme Court.

Then Benjamin Franklin had come out with

an amusing idea. "Two modes of chusing the judges have been mentioned," he drawled, "to wit, by the legislature and by the executive." Why not copy an old "Scotch mode, in which the nomination proceeded from the lawyers, who always selected the ablest of the profession in order to get rid of him and share his practice among themselves."

No one took the suggestion seriously. And when Madison proposed the judges be appointed by the Senate, it was agreed to as a sort of compromise.

But now, after the small states had obtained equal votes in the Senate, Madison changed his tune. He wanted the judges appointed by the president, with the "advice and consent" of the Senate. The big states agreed. The small states objected. Both groups, however, put their arguments in terms of whether president or Senate would be better able to choose good judges.

"The Senate," said Morris of Pennsylvania, "must take the character of candidates from the flattering pictures drawn by their friends." To the contrary, insisted Ellsworth of Connecticut, the president "will be more open to caresses and intrigues than the Senate."

Madison himself was a little franker. If the Senate, with the small states voting equally,

113

should do the choosing, "the judges might be appointed by a minority of the people." "Moreover," he added, with an appeal to the South, "it would throw the appointments entirely into the hands of the Northern states."

But there was no real squabbling now. And though the appointment of the Supreme Court was left for a while in the Senate's hands, it was later given to the president, without a single murmur of protest. In spite of Mason's bad prediction of Senate "complaisance," toward all presidential appointments, the small states were satisfied with the Senate's right to reject whatever judges the president might choose.

There was no discussion at all about giving the judges life terms on the Supreme Court. The judges, after all, were to be the final guardians of the rights the Constitution was meant to protect. They, above all, must not be swayed by political prejudice nor turned aside by popular whim. Of course, in extreme cases, they were to be subject to impeachment, so their terms were described as "during good behaviour." But, as Mason said, when a similar term was proposed for the president, "an executive during good behaviour is a softer name only for an executive for life."

And even with a life term, there was no objection to forbidding Congress from cutting the judges' salaries while they held office. Congress must not be able to browbeat the judges with threats to reduce their pay.

It was even suggested that Congress should also be unable to raise judges' salaries, for fear of its using this method to bribe the Supreme Court. But, as Franklin said, "money may become plentier," and the buying power of a set salary would then be automatically reduced. And to Madison's idea of "taking, for a standard, wheat or some thing of permanent value," Morris replied: "The value of money may not only alter but the state of society may alter. The amount of salaries must always be regulated by the manners and the style of living in a country." So the notion of forbidding increases in judges' salaries was dropped, even at the risk of Congressional bribes.

But the delegates did not foresee nor guard against another possible method of influencing Supreme Court decisions. They put no limit on the number of judges the president might appoint. And to this day, the Constitution does not say that the Court must be made up of more than one nor less than a hundred judges.

With the outline of the new government sketched in for the time being, the delegates

115

turned to consider the powers to be given it. Surprisingly—at least in the light of theories widely held today about a conflict between state and national power—there was nothing much to be said. Both large and small states had taken for granted that the new government was to be a strong government, with power to make and enforce laws for the nation as a whole. Certainly, there was to be no more of this interstate conference stuff, as under the Confederation.

To bother, therefore, to list all the kinds of laws the new Congress could pass seemed, if not entirely unnecessary, no more than a minor detail. It would be a waste of time to attempt it on the floor of the Convention. What was far more important, now, was to see to it that the states be kept from interfering with the national government.

Accordingly, Sherman—although he had fought for equal state votes in the Senate—moved that the state governments be restricted to "matters of internal police," and those "wherein the general welfare of the United States is not concerned." Only Congress should "make laws binding on the people of the United States in all cases which may concern the common interests of the Union."

Morris objected that even this would leave
116

the states too much freedom. "The internal police, as it would be called and understood by the states, ought to be infringed in many cases, as in the case of paper money and other tricks by which citizens of other states may be affected."

And it was Bedford, of all the members—the same Bedford who had earlier shocked the Convention with his fiery defense of the "rights" of the small states—who then changed Sherman's motion so that it satisfied Morris. He moved, and Morris promptly seconded, that Congress "legislate in all cases for the general interests of the Union, and also in those to which the states are severally incompetent or in which the harmony of the United States may be interrupted by the exercise of individual legislation."

This would give the new government, as Randolph put it, "the power of violating all the laws and constitutions of the states, and of intermeddling with their police." It was nevertheless accepted almost unanimously.

Even so, the delegates were not yet satisfied that the states would be kept in their proper places. The idea of letting Congress veto state laws was raised again. But that was to be one job of the judges; and would take up too much of Congress' time.

At least, then, all state officers must be made to take oaths to support the Constitution. There was no objection to this. It would bind the states morally, if not legally, not to trespass on national territory.

But when similar oaths were suggested for national officers, Wilson stood up in protest. He had never, he said, been "fond of oaths, considering them as a left handed security only. A good government does not need them, and a bad one can not or ought not to be supported. I am afraid they might too much trammel the members of the existing government in case future alterations should be necessary."

Again, however, Wilson's was a voice crying in the wilderness. Gorham did not quite answer him, in replying that "a constitutional alteration of the Constitution can never be regarded as a breach of the Constitution, or of any oath to support it." And the other delegates, without a dissenting vote, decided to require the oath from national as well as state officers.

But the Convention was not yet through protecting the national government against the separate states. The recent riots in Massachusetts had warned of another danger. The people themselves, if they could not get what they wanted through their established governments, might rise in rebellion, first against state, then against national laws.

As Gorham said—and his words have a twentieth century touch—"an enterprising citizen might erect the standard of monarchy in a particular state, might gather together partizans from all quarters, might extend his views from state to state, and threaten to establish a tyranny over the whole, and the general government be compelled to remain an inactive witness of its own destruction."

To guard against this, the nation would have to "guarantee" to each state a republican form of government. "The object," as Wilson put it, "is merely to secure the states against dangerous commotions, insurrections, and rebellions." And Randolph and Madison, to make the meaning perfectly clear, wanted the provisions written: "that no state be at liberty to form any other than a republican government." But this was a little blunt. So the softer "guarantee" was kept, and protection "against invasion" was added, in order to make the section sound like a favor to the states.

One final rivet was welded into the Constitution to strengthen the framework of national supremacy. Not only the Constitution itself, but also all laws passed by Congress were pro-

119

claimed "the supreme law of the land." And "the judges in every state" were ordered to follow this supreme law, "any thing in the constitution or laws of any state to the contrary notwithstanding."

But even with this, the state judges could not be trusted too far. They had refused to pay much attention to such laws as were passed by the Confederation Congress. Many of the delegates had been members of that Congress, and they had learned their lesson.

As Randolph remarked, a trifle bitterly, "the courts of the states can not be trusted with the administration of the national laws." Yet it would be asking too much to expect the Supreme Court itself to hear every case that might come up under those laws. So, to make sure national laws would be properly enforced, Congress was given the right, on its own initiative, to set up "inferior courts" throughout the nation.

* * *

With the new government thus safely guarded against interference or disobedience by the states, it came time to put the whole plan in the form of a constitution. A committee "of detail" was quickly chosen. Geographically, its five members represented each part of the Union. But the small states, satisfied now with their equal votes in the Senate, made no effort to be represented for themselves.

From New England were chosen Gorham of Massachusetts and Ellsworth of Connecticut. From the South were Randolph of Virginia and Rutledge of South Carolina. Wilson of Pennsylvania talked for the middle states. To these men went the task of preparing the first draft of the great document.

The committee, however, did more than merely round into shape the resolutions that the Convention had passed. It enlarged some of these resolutions and added some new provisions of its own. So for more than a month after the committee had reported, the delegates continued to discuss old and new provisions, and some others that had been forgotten, before the Constitution was turned over to another committee to be put in final form.

Among the new provisions written in by the committee of detail were rules to govern the proceedings of the House and Senate. A complicated scheme was set up for the Senate to handle disputes between the states over Western territory. The nation and the states were forbidden to hand out titles of nobility.

On the legal side, the committee listed the kinds of cases the Supreme Court should hear,

121

including "all cases arising" under laws passed by Congress. But in order to lighten the Supreme Court's load, the right was given Congress to let some of these cases be tried first in whatever lower courts Congress might set up.

The committee also took a few more shots at what little was left of state independence. Each state was ordered to give "full faith and credit" to the laws and court decisions of every other state. And each state was forbidden to take from the citizens of other states whatever "privileges and immunities" it gave to its own citizens.

But perhaps most important of all, the committee enlarged on the powers of the new government. Not satisfied with the general description of these powers which the Convention had rather casually accepted, maybe afraid that the general words would be too narrowly interpreted, the committee proceeded to make a list of all the kinds of laws it could think of, that Congress might want to pass.

First on the list were taxes of all sorts, including "duties, imposts, and excises." Next came laws "to regulate commerce with foreign nations, and among the several states." Taxation and regulation were to be the chief powers and duties of the new government—as they are of any government.

122

Then the list included laws "to coin money;—to establish post-offices; to borrow money;" and farther down on the list, "to make war; to raise armies; to build and equip fleets." In between came various minor laws, such as to naturalize immigrants, to punish counterfeiters, and—of more importance in 1787—to punish "piracies and felonies committed on the high seas."

At the end of the list, as a final catch-all, came all laws "necessary and proper" to make effective any of the laws named above or any "other powers" intended for the new government. The committee apparently was taking no chances.

But when the list was put before the Convention the other delegates were not quite satisfied. To most of the laws included, such as those to regulate commerce, they agreed without any discussion at all. But they wanted the list made longer. And to a few of its parts they objected strenuously.

The committee had given Congress the power "to emit bills of credit" as well as to borrow money. The specter of more paper money than the states were already printing was too much for some of the delegates. Said Gouverneur Morris, his eye on a balanced budget, "the monied interest will oppose the plan of government

123

if paper emissions be not prohibited."

Even Ellsworth, who had served on the committee, thought it "a favorable moment to shut and bar the door against paper money." And Wilson, too, agreed that to do so would have "a most salutary influence on the credit of the United States."

But Mason, though he himself felt "a mortal hatred to paper money," reminded the Convention that "the late war could not have been carried on, had such a prohibition existed." And Mercer—rare among the delegates—confessed that, personally, he was "a friend to paper money," and warned the others that, if they wanted the Constitution ratified, it would be "impolitic to excite the opposition of all those who are friends to paper money." So paper money was not ruled out entirely. Instead, the committee's words were changed to allow Congress "to borrow money on the credit of the United States."

There was objection to giving Congress the unlimited right to raise armies. Afraid of a military dictatorship, Gerry felt that a standing army in time of peace would be "dangerous to liberty, and unnecessary even for so great an extent of country as this." So, to lessen the danger, Congress was forbidden to appropriate money for the army any more than two years ahead.

Then, the carrying on of a war being the president's job as commander-in-chief, Congress was allowed to "declare" war but not to "make" it. But most of the objections to the committee's list were not that it gave Congress too many powers. Instead, the delegates were by no means sure that it granted enough.

Control of bankruptcies was put on the list, with practically no discussion. Here, again, the states could not be left to their own devices. For the states had been treating debtors much too kindly.

In order "to promote the progress of science and useful arts," the right to grant patents and copyrights was added to the list. So was the right to establish a seat of government for the new nation. But the right to found a university was turned down as "not necessary," inasmuch as Congress could, if it wanted to, build a university at the national capital.

The right "to establish post roads" was attached to the right to set up post offices. Of course, the delegates assumed that mail would be carried along the highways. Even in inventor Franklin's mind, there was no thought of railroads nor of airplanes. But it was Franklin who suggested that Congress be given the right

125

to cut canals, which was voted down after Sherman had objected that "the expence in such cases will fall on the United States, and the benefit accrue to the places where the canals may be cut."

Then Madison brought up, for the second time, an interesting idea. He had wanted before to give Congress the right "to grant charters of incorporation in cases where the public good may require them, and the authority of a single state may be incompetent." Now he pointed out that this would help Congress keep national trade free from state interference.

Wilson agreed that allowing a company, especially a transportation company, to set itself up under national law, instead of under state law, was "necessary to prevent a *state* from obstructing the *general* welfare." But King was afraid that Madison's proposal would let Congress hand out "mercantile monopolies." He had visions of government-favored companies destroying the free competition of private industry.

Moreover, Congress already had the power "to regulate commerce among the several states." And Wilson, who had helped to draft that phrase, thought that even the right to grant monopolies was "already included in the power

126

to regulate trade." The others, while not agreeing with Wilson that regulation should go that far, did feel it went far enough to let them turn down Madison's proposal. National incorporation, as another aid to national control of national commerce, seemed, as King had said, "unnecessary."

And still, the long list of specific laws that Congress could pass was not allowed to stand alone. For the committee, in making the list, had left out the Convention's broad permission to Congress to "legislate in all cases for the general interests of the Union."

But in the final draft of the Constitution, the "general interests of the Union" were not forgotten. And today, at the very head of the list, stands the right to use any national funds "to provide for the common defence and general welfare of the United States."

In spite of the fact that the word "national" was not used once in the entire document, a real national government was now assured. Congress had been given every power the delegates thought would ever be needed to keep complete control in the central government. From "general welfare" at the top of the list, to "all laws necessary and proper" at the bottom, nothing of any importance seemed to be missing. And to make assurance doubly sure, every law that Congress might pass had been labelled "the supreme law of the land." This, at least, should put the states back in their proper places. This should teach them to keep their fingers out of national affairs.

VII

A GOVERNMENT OF MEN—NOT OF LAWS

WITH a strong national government made certain, with such tremendous powers given to Congress, the delegates began to worry a little about the men who were to make the national laws. The state legislatures, with their wild ideas, seemed pretty well bottled up. The state courts, with their contempt for law and order, seemed effectively put under thumb. But how about the men who were to wield the national bludgeon? How about the members of Congress themselves?

The Constitution itself would be useless to accomplish its purpose if the wrong kind of men got into office under it. "It is a great mistake," said Mercer, "to suppose that the paper we are to propose will govern the United States. It is the men whom it will bring into the government and interest in maintaining it."

It had been voted earlier that no senator or congressman might be appointed, during his term in Congress, to any other national office, whether as ambassador, judge, commissioner, or cabinet member. This was done with the idea, as Rutledge put it, of "preserving the legislature as pure as possible, by shutting the door against

131

appointments of its own members to offices, which is one source of its corruption."

But even then, there had been plenty of opposition. King felt that "we are refining too much. Such a restriction on the members will discourage merit." Moreover, he had added—and he might have been talking today—even if "no member shall himself be eligible to any office, will this restrain him from availing himself of the same means which would gain appointment for himself, to gain them for his son, his brother, or any other object of his partiality?"

And Madison had warned that even if the members themselves were disqualified, "candidates for office will hover round the seat of government or be found among the residents there, and practise all the means of courting the favor of the members." He, too, was afraid that the restriction would add to "the backwardness of the best citizens to engage in the legislative service," and he preferred to risk some corruption if necessary to get "the wisest and most worthy citizens" into Congress.

Moreover, Hamilton, with his usual frankness, had come right out in the open with his reasons. "We must take man as we find him," he had commented matter-of-factly, "and if we expect him to serve the public, must interest his passions in doing so. A reliance on pure patriotism has been the source of many of our errors."

At the time, these arguments had gone to waste. But now that so much power had been put in the hands of Congress, they began to take effect. Even Mercer, who favored paper money, did not want to take a chance on keeping "the best part of our citizens" out of Congress. The restriction on appointments, he feared, would lead "all the most influential men to stay at home."

Pinckney added that the restriction would be an insult to members of Congress. He wanted it toned down, following an earlier idea of Madison's, so that members would be barred from offices that were created, or for which the salary was raised, only during their terms in Congress. He had hopes, he said, that the Senate, at least, would become "a school of public ministers, a nursery of statesmen."

Gerry replied that he was "not so fond of those productions as to wish to establish nurseries for them." And Mason, who also liked the restriction, sarcastically proposed "to strike out the whole section, as a more effectual expedient for encouraging that exotic corruption which might not otherwise thrive so well in the American soil."

But taunts such as these did not deter the other

133

delegates. They were impressed by the argument that to get "the best citizens" into Congress, its members must have a chance to be appointed to something higher. Accordingly, the restriction was toned down as Pinckney had urged, after Pinckney himself, a bit oratorically, pointed to "the policy of the Romans, in making the temple of virtue the road to the temple of fame."

Yet if certain men were to be encouraged to enter Congress, there were others who must be barred. The Revolution was not long past. Memory of the Tories was fresh in the minds of the delegates. Men with foreign leanings and foreign prejudices must not be allowed to have a hand in running the new government.

Of course, all senators and congressmen were to be citizens. But most of the delegates felt that citizenship was not enough. They wanted no man to help in making laws for the nation who had not been a citizen of the nation for a safe number of years.

Morris spoke of "the danger of admitting strangers into our public councils." Mason, too, did "not chuse to let foreigners and adventurers make laws for us and govern us." For example, he explained, "if persons among us attached to Great Britain should work themselves

134

into our councils, a turn might be given to our affairs and particularly to our commercial regulations which might have pernicious consequences."

Gerry's fears went still farther. "Every one knows," he warned, "the vast sums laid out in Europe for secret services." And Butler, being himself no native, said he spoke from experience. "If I had been called into public life within a short time after my coming to America, my foreign habits, opinions and attachments would have rendered me an improper agent in public affairs."

Madison, on the other hand, did not want to be too strict. He thought the dangers were being exaggerated, and reminded the Convention that "instances are rare of a foreigner being elected by the people within any short space after his coming among us." And Hamilton also felt that "the advantage of encouraging foreigners is obvious and admitted."

Then Wilson pointed out that three of Pennsylvania's delegates, including himself, were not natives. Moreover, "almost all the general officers of the Pennsylvania line of the late army were foreigners. And no complaint has ever been made against their fidelity or their merit." He was especially bothered by "the possibility,

135

if the ideas of some gentlemen should be pursued, of my being incapacitated from holding a place under the very Constitution which I have shared in the trust of making."

But at least one of those gentlemen refused to be put off. "We should not," replied Morris, "be polite at the expence of prudence. It is said that some tribes of Indians carry their hospitality so far as to offer to strangers their wives and daughters. Is this a proper model for us? I would admit them to my house, I would invite them to my table, would provide for them comfortable lodgings; but would not carry the complaisance so far as to bed them with my wife. I would let them worship at the same altar, but do not choose to make priests of them."

Morris carried his point. It was voted that seven years of citizenship be required for the House, and nine years for the Senate.

Then Rutledge wanted to add that each member of Congress must also have lived for a number of years in the state that elected him. He thought that "an emigrant from New England to South Carolina or Georgia would know little of its affairs." But he was shouted down. Remember, said Read of little Delaware, that "we are now forming a *national* government."

Yet if recent immigrants from foreign shores

were to be excluded from Congress, why not keep out another dangerous group of men? Why not keep out the poor and the debtors who had been raising hob in the state legislatures? Why not make sure that every man who had a hand in making the national laws was a property-owner? As Gerry said, "if property be one object of government, provisions to secure it cannot be improper."

Mason moved that a clause be written into the Constitution "requiring certain qualifications of landed property, and disqualifying persons having unsettled accounts with or being indebted to the United States." Not one of the delegates was shocked at the notion of barring the poor from the national government.

Only Dickinson got up to "doubt the policy of interweaving into a republican constitution a veneration for wealth." And Franklin observed that even "if honesty is often the companion of wealth, and if poverty is exposed to peculiar temptation, it is not less true that the possession of property increases the desire of more property. Some of the greatest rogues I was ever acquainted with were the richest rogues."

But there were other and more effective objections to Mason's motion. If all men with unsettled government accounts were kept out of

137

Congress, "what," asked Morris, "will be done with those patriotic citizens who have lent money or services or property to their country, without having been yet able to obtain a liquidation of their claims?" He was talking, of course, for those who still held unpaid notes or bonds of the Confederation.

Moreover, he added, "the last clause, relating to public debtors will exclude every importing merchant." For the government, naturally, would put tariffs on imported goods. And each importer who had not paid these taxes up to the minute would owe money to the United States and be barred from a seat in Congress.

The same clause, Pinckney pointed out, "will exclude persons who have purchased confiscated property, or should purchase Western territory, and might be some obstacle to the sale of the latter." For these buyers of government land could not be expected to pay the whole price immediately in cash.

As for making every member of Congress be a land-owner, there were even stronger objections. This, as King put it, "would exclude the monied interest," whose wealth was in securities and investments instead of land. And Morris went so far as to call the idea "a scheme of the landed against the monied interest."

138

Then Madison put his finger on the chief difficulty. "Landed possessions," he said, "are no certain evidence of real wealth. Many enjoy them to a great extent who are more in debt than they are worth." Furthermore—with a shot at the farmers in the state legislatures— "the unjust laws of the states have proceeded more from this class of men than any others."

The trouble was, according to Madison, that "if a small quantity of land should be made the standard, it will be no security; if a large one, it will exclude the proper representatives of those classes of citizens who are not landholders."

Langdon, who had just arrived from New Hampshire, brought up another telling point. When it came to getting the Constitution ratified, the property qualifications might "render the system unacceptable to the people." And Rutledge, although he approved of such qualifications, realized "the danger on one side of displeasing the people by making them high, and on the other of rendering them nugatory by making them low."

So the Convention, after having once voted to keep poor men and debtors out of Congress, finally decided that the restriction would be, not improper, but impractical. In the first place,

139

there was, as Madison phrased it, "the difficulty of forming any uniform standard." In the second place, there was the danger of having the Constitution turned down by the people.

But there was still another way to stop Congress from turning its vast powers in the wrong direction. The "respectable" Senate was, of course, to be the first guard against any wild, popular laws that got through the House. Yet, too much reliance could not be placed on the Senate. It was, after all, to be elected by the state legislatures which were certainly no great respecters of property rights.

How about, then, digging up from the original Randolph plan a veto power for the Supreme Court? The Supreme Court could be trusted, if anyone could be trusted, to put its foot down on bad laws. If it had to wait for a chance to call them unconstitutional, that might be too late.

There are people today who think the Court was never intended to call acts of Congress unconstitutional. They say the idea was invented by John Marshall, the great chief justice who first used that power. And certainly, nowhere in the Constitution is the power written down in black and white.

But most of the men who wrote the Constitution expected the Court to have that power, and use it. Gerry talked of the Court's "exposition of the laws, which involves a power of deciding on their constitutionality." Madison said that "a law violating a constitution established by the people themselves will be considered by the judges as null and void." Martin realized that "the constitutionality of laws will come before the judges in their proper official character." And Mason took it for granted the Court "can declare an unconstitutional law void."

True, Mercer was frank to "disapprove of the doctrine that the judges as expositors of the Constitution should have authority to declare a law void." And Dickinson, too, thought "no such power ought to exist." But even these men merely disliked the power. They did not deny it was there.

And now there was an attempt to give the judges still more power. Why not let the Court, either by itself or else along with the president, veto all acts passed by Congress before they became law? As Wilson put it: "Laws may be unjust, may be unwise, may be dangerous, may be destructive; and yet may not be so unconstitutional as to justify the judges in refusing to give them effect."

Madison had been pulling hard for a judicial

141

veto from the very beginning. He thought it would be "useful to the community at large as an additional check against a pursuit of those unwise and unjust measures which constitute so great a portion of our calamities." And Mason also was afraid that "notwithstanding the precautions" already taken in setting up the national legislature, "it will still so much resemble that of the individual states, that it must be expected frequently to pass unjust and pernicious laws."

Then Morris made perfectly clear what sort of laws Wilson, Madison, and Mason had united in labelling "unjust." "Emissions of paper money," he warned, "largesses to the people, a remission of debts, and similar measures will at some times be popular, and will be pushed for that reason."

So far as the president's veto is concerned, Morris predicted, Congress "will contrive to soften down the president." And, as Wilson had pointed out, there would be no excuse for the Supreme Court to declare these laws unconstitutional. Morris therefore agreed that the Supreme Court should be given a real veto power as a "strong barrier against the instability of legislative assemblies."

But most of the delegates balked at going

quite this far. Not that they, any more than the rest, wanted paper money laws and other popular measures. Not that they thought the Supreme Court could call such laws unconstitutional merely because they might be "unjust." But these men were afraid that a Supreme Court veto would drag the Court into politics, destroy its dignity, weakening instead of strengthening its power.

"I disapprove," said Sherman, "of judges meddling in politics and parties." Gerry thought "making statesmen of the judges" was a poor idea. Strong agreed that "the power of making ought to be kept distinct from that of expounding the laws." And Martin called the whole business "a dangerous innovation."

Gorham could not see why the Court would have "any peculiar knowledge of the mere policy of public measures." And Rutledge went so far as to brand the judges "of all men the most unfit" to have a hand in the making of laws.

So the Supreme Court veto was once more rejected, but by a very close vote. For many of the delegates still wondered whether the Supreme Court might not be their best protection against the kind of laws they did not want Congress to pass.

Then Morris, still fighting against such laws,

143

revived the idea of giving the president an absolute veto that could not be overruled by Congress. "Encroachments of the popular branch of the government," he insisted, "ought to be guarded against." And the Senate could not be relied on to act as a brake on the House, because even "the most virtuous citizens will often, as members of a legislative body, concur in measures which afterwards in their private capacity they will be ashamed of."

By this time it was getting well into August. Although Langdon and Gilman had finally shown up from New Hampshire, the other delegates, after three long months of the Convention, were growing restless. A few of them, feeling that the important part of their work was done, had already started to leave Philadelphia.

Rutledge, as Madison described him, "complained much of the tediousness of the proceedings." He spoke of "the impatience of the public and the extreme anxiety of many members of the Convention to bring the business to an end."

So nobody paid much attention to Morris' lingering worries about giving the president a stronger veto. All the delegates sympathized with his wish to guard the new government

144

against the wrong kind of laws. All of them knew, as he knew, that the men who held office under it would determine the course of that government.

But they felt that they had already set up enough "checks and balances" to do the job. They felt the ship of state would be safe from irresponsible pilots. And they were eager to get on, get finished, and get home.

VIII

THE LAST PIECE IN THE PICTURE

O NE important problem had been plaguing the Convention from the very beginning. Wilson called it "the most difficult of all on which we have had to decide." It was the puzzle of how to elect the president.

The original Randolph plan gave the election to Congress. And when the delegates went over the plan, as a "committee of the whole," they left this provision unchanged. Wilson talked vaguely for election by the people. And Gerry was afraid that Congress "and the candidates will bargain, and play into one another's hands."

But Gerry also felt that the people themselves would be "too little informed" and too "liable to deceptions" to be trusted with the election. And when Wilson suggested that the people elect electors, who in turn would elect the president, nobody was much impressed. It took the Convention almost three months to come around to this early idea of Wilson's.

The Randolph plan also made the president ineligible for a second term. Sherman did not like "throwing out of office the man best qualified to execute its duties." But Mason answered that a chance for re-election would put "a temptation

149

on the side of the executive to intrigue with the legislature." And the other delegates agreed with him.

The length of the president's one term was left blank in the Randolph plan. The "committee" wrote in seven years, decided on one president instead of three, approved the section as it stood, and let it go at that.

But after the representation fight was finished, and as soon as such vast powers had been given Congress, a few of the delegates started to worry about giving Congress the right to pick the president, too. For the president's job was not only to enforce laws passed by Congress. He was also to put a stop to the bad ones by vetoing them.

Morris, in particular, was afraid the president would become a bus-boy for Congress. Though no special friend of the people, he preferred that the people elect the president. He, like Gerry, had a hunch that otherwise the president might trade his election for a blank cheque to Congress to pass any laws it pleased.

Sherman, speaking for the small states, replied that the people "will generally vote for some man in their own state, and the largest state will have the best chance for the appointment." And Pinckney was afraid that demagogues would

150

control a popular election. The people, he said, "will be led by a few active and designing men."

"This," Morris answered, "might happen in a small district. It can never happen throughout the continent." There were, after all, no telegraph wires and no radios in 1787.

It was at this point that Mason cried out: "It would be as unnatural to refer the choice of a proper character for chief magistrate to the people, as it would to refer a trial of colours to a blind man." And the Convention, apparently agreeing, voted unanimously to leave the election with Congress.

But Morris was not yet beaten. Two days later he was up again, insisting that "one great object of the executive is to control the legislature;" and that the president "should be the guardian of the people, even of the lower classes, against legislative tyranny." He was still sure that in a national election the people "can not be influenced by those little combinations and those momentary lies, which often decide popular elections within a narrow sphere."

Morris' fear that Congress would put the president under its thumb, and keep him there, began to spread through the Convention. King revived Wilson's early notion of using electors. Paterson—his bitter enemy a few days back—

151

agreed heartily with King. I perceive," grinned Wilson, "with pleasure that the idea is gaining ground."

Madison joined the band-wagon for election by electors. He pointed out that the plan could be worded to give the South extra votes for its slaves, who, of course, would not be allowed to vote in a direct election by the people. And suddenly the Convention switched, and adopted the elector plan.

But instead of letting the people choose the electors, as Wilson had intended, the choice was given to the state legislatures as perhaps a little more safe. This, however, brought up the old question of representation. How many electors could each state choose?

Before the large and small states had time to square off for another fight, Georgia complained of a second hitch in the plan. To send men way up from Georgia, just to meet and elect a president, would mean "extreme inconveniency and considerable expence." The Convention switched right back to election by Congress.

Other and odder schemes were proposed from time to time. Gerry suggested letting the governors of the states elect the president. But Randolph blew this plan to pieces with a reminder that the president, among other things, must "defend national rights against state encroachments." And the governors, he added, of all people, "will not cherish the great oak which is to reduce them to paltry shrubs."

Later, Gerry moved that, instead of the governors, the state legislatures elect the president. "The noes," wrote Madison, "were so predominant that the states were not counted."

Another scheme was to let the people elect but make each voter cast two ballots, one of them for a candidate who did not come from the voter's own state. Madison—wise politician that he was—predicted that "each citizen, after having given his vote for his favorite fellow citizen, would throw away his second on some obscure citizen of another state, in order to ensure the object of his first choice." Yet this idea was made a part of the plan that was finally adopted.

Dickinson, at one point, suggested that the people of each state elect "its best citizen," and that Congress then choose from among the thirteen candidates. And Wilson came out seriously with the notion of giving the election to a few members of Congress, the members themselves to be picked by pulling their names out of a hat.

These and other schemes showed, at least, that sentiment was growing stronger against direct election of the president by Congress. Madison

153

cut straight to the root of this sentiment. The state legislatures, he said, have "a strong propensity to a variety of pernicious measures;" it is up to Congress "to control this propensity;" and it is up to the president to control Congress "so far as it may be infected with a similar propensity." But, once give Congress the election of the president, "and this controlling purpose may be defeated."

Madison, for one, had made up his mind that, "with all its imperfections," he liked election by the people best. And this, in spite of the fact that it would give the more thickly settled Northern states a big advantage. As a Southerner, he announced, "I am willing to make the sacrifice."

On the other hand, sentiment was equally strong against election of the president by the people. Gerry still insisted that "a popular election in this case is radically vicious." Among other things, the election might be controlled by a small, united, national group. For example, there was the Order of the Cincinnati, the ex-soldiers of the Revolution. "My respect for the characters composing this Society," said Gerry, "can not blind me to the danger and impropriety of throwing such a power into their hands."

Caught, thus, between two fires, the Convention let the whole matter drop for a while. And

154

when the committee of detail was asked to prepare the first draft of the Constitution, election of the president was still in the hands of Congress.

In the meantime, the delegates had been shuttling back and forth on another question. Should the president, however he was elected, be eligible for a second term? So long as he was to be elected by Congress, the answer was usually no. The idea was to keep him from playing up to Congress during his first term, in order to get a second one.

Accordingly, arguments against election by Congress were coupled with arguments against the wisdom of restricting the president to one term. Morris, for instance, wanted to give him a chance for a second term as a "reward," and also as a "motive to good behavior" during his first one. Taking away this chance and this motive was, as Morris put it, "saying to him, 'make hay while the sun shines'."

Morris got his point across. The Convention voted to make the president, even though elected by Congress, eligible for a second term.

But should the terms, then, be as long as seven years? An effort was immediately made to cut the terms to three or four years.

Dr. McClurg of Virginia, who had said very little up to now, was worried by the thought of

155

what might happen if Congress were allowed, not only to elect the president, but to re-elect him. He therefore moved that, instead of shortening the president's term, it be stretched to a life term. Not entirely serious, his real purpose was to stress the danger of making the president re-eligible.

But Morris was not phased in the slightest. "This," he chortled, "is the way to get a good government." And Broome of Delaware seconded McClurg's motion.

Mason, by now, was genuinely alarmed. After all, Hamilton and a few others had wanted to give the president a life term before. Apparently, the notion could not be laughed off, despite the fact that it would be "an easy step to hereditary monarchy."

But Madison thought that a king, although he did not want one, would be even less dangerous than a government run entirely by Congress. In the states themselves, from which so many bad laws had been coming, the governors were "in general little more than cyphers." And the brief excitement quieted down as soon as McClurg's motion had been defeated.

Yet, the motion itself and Madison's comment served their purpose. The delegates began to see that a president elected by Congress, and open to re-election, might well result in a government completely controlled by Congress.

Morris realized that his plans for re-election of the president, with which he hoped eventually to take the election out of Congress' hands, were losing ground. He got to his feet again to warn that keeping the president from a second term would "tempt him to make the most of the short space of time allotted him, to accumulate wealth and provide for his friends." But Randolph, who liked election by Congress and therefore opposed a second term for the president, thought there would be a greater "temptation to court a re-appointment" by bowing down to Congress during the first term.

All right, said Morris, if you really want your president not to be a flunkey to Congress, "let him not be impeachable." This was a new and bold idea, for it had been taken for granted the president, no matter how elected, could be impeached. "Shall any man," demanded Mason, "be above justice?"

Then Franklin, witty as usual, put a new slant on the impeachment question. He remarked that impeachment might turn out to be a favor to the president. Otherwise, a really bad one would probably be assassinated, and "not only deprived of his life but of the opportunity of

157

vindicating his character."

Even Morris could not quite answer this. He made the rare confession that "my opinion has been changed." The notion of putting the president above impeachment was not raised again.

But the feeling against re-election of the president was growing stronger. It turned, for a while, into suggestions that the president be given a longer term. Martin mentioned eleven years. Gerry raised it to fifteen. King—according to Madison, "as a caricature of the previous motions"—went as high as twenty. "This," said King, drily, "is the medium life of princes."

But Williamson was worried by all this long term talk. "The president," he warned, "will spare no pains to keep himself in for life, and will then lay a train of succession for his children."

Morris, on the other hand, refused to be bothered by these suggestions. He wanted to give the president a chance for more than one term, but a long term suited him even better than a short one. Even with the president re-eligible, he said, "some leader of a party will always covet his seat, will perplex his administration, will cabal with the legislature, till he succeeds in supplanting him."

158

Ellsworth put the same idea in plainer language. He might have been talking about any president today. "There will be *outs* as well as *ins,*" he predicted. "His administration therefore will be attacked and misrepresented."

But soon discussion swung back to the real question. Should, or should not the president be eligible for a second term? Yes, answered Wilson, who was fighting on Morris' side. Otherwise, the president, "in the very prime of life," would be "cast aside like a useless hulk."

Morris followed up this argument. Should we, he asked, give the president "the benefit of experience, and then deprive ourselves of the use of it?"

But the tide was turning rapidly, and Morris knew it. Congress, apparently, was to elect the president. If so, it would not be safe to give Congress the chance to bribe the president by promising to re-elect him.

It was Franklin who clinched the point with a clever twist. "In free governments," he said, looking sideways at Morris, "the rulers are the servants, and the people their superiors." So, to send presidents back among the plain people after one term in office "is not to *degrade* but to *promote* them."

Immediately, the Convention restored the

159

clause making presidents ineligible for a second term. And in the first draft of the Constitution, which gave the election to Congress, the president was to hold his place for seven years, and no more.

So far as the presidential puzzle was concerned, the Convention was now right back where it started. And after the committee of detail had written out the first draft of the document, a new problem stared the delegates in the face. If Congress was to elect the president, how should Congress vote? Should House and Senate get together and cast their votes all in a bunch, so that a senator's vote would be worth no more than a representative's? Or should each house of Congress vote separately in the hope that both, sooner or later, would agree on one man?

The big states were quick to point out the difficulties involved in taking two separate ballots. House and Senate might never be able to find a president that suited them both. "Great delay and confusion would ensue," said Gorham of Massachusetts.

The small states, however, were not fooled by the "delay and confusion" argument. "A joint ballot," replied Dayton of New Jersey, "would in fact give the appointment to the House."

160

And giving the appointment to the House would mean that the big states could pick their own president.

With another fight brewing, Morris decided the time was ripe to try, once more, to take the election away from Congress entirely. Persuaded there was no hope of giving it to the people, he went back to Wilson's plan of using electors. He was voted down, but only by the margin of one state. The Convention was gradually coming around to agree with Morris that the president should not be named by Congress.

Headed for another stale-mate, and anxious to get home, the delegates turned the whole bothersome problem over to a committee. Morris was on the committee. And at last he had his way.

The committee, largely under Morris' direction, came out with a complicated scheme to satisfy both the large and small states, and yet to give the election directly neither to Congress nor the people. And except for two or three minor changes, that scheme is still, today, a part of the Constitution.

According to the scheme, the people of each state were to vote for presidential electors. Each state was to choose as many electors as its total

161

number of representatives and senators — in other words, its number of representatives plus two. This, of course, gave the large states a big advantage.

Next, the electors chosen in each state were to get together in that state. Each elector was then to vote for two men for president. But no elector might vote for more than one man from his own state.

The votes of the electors in all the states were then to be sealed and sent to the national Senate to be counted. If more than half the electors had voted for any one candidate the man with the most votes was to be proclaimed president.

But if no man had received the votes of more than half the electors, or if two men were tied with that many votes—for each elector would have voted twice—then the small states were to get their chance. For then, the Senate was to choose the president from among the leading candidates. And in the Senate, of course, the smallest state would have as many votes as the largest.

Finally, the candidate who was runner-up in the vote that determined the president was to become, in turn, the vice-president, and preside over the Senate. Both president and vice-president were then to be eligible for more than one term. And because of this, their terms were shortened from seven years to four.

In spite of all its careful compromises, the committee's plan brought immediate squawks from some of the large states' delegates. Pinckney and Rutledge of South Carolina, Williamson of North Carolina, and Mason of Virginia were far from satisfied with the lion's share of the electoral votes. Using almost identical words, all four protested that the plan would throw the election "in fact, into the hands of the Senate." This was bad prediction. Only twice in the nation's history has the electoral vote failed to determine the president.

Wilson of Pennsylvania, too, thought the plan would make the president "the minion of the Senate." For the Senate, after maybe electing the president, was to have the right to turn down any appointments he made. "He cannot," Wilson reminded the delegates, "even appoint a tide-waiter without the Senate."

Wilson and Randolph wanted to know why, when the electoral vote was not decisive, the final choice was not given to Congress as a whole, instead of to the Senate. "The Senate was preferred," Morris replied, "because fewer can then say to the president, you owe your appointment to us." Of course, giving fewer men

163

strings on the president was only one reason. The other was to get the small states to support the plan.

For a day or two, the grumblings continued. A few variations were suggested, such as putting the final choice in the hands of six senators and seven representatives, elected themselves by Congress. But the notion of using electors, to start with, now seemed to have taken everyone's fancy.

Yet, leaving the last choice to the Senate might, as Wilson had warned, be dangerous. Part of the president's job was to appoint judges, ambassadors, consuls, cabinet members, and countless other government officials. But every one of these appointments had to be confirmed, and could be blocked, by the Senate. And a Senate-elected president might feel he must knuckle down to the Senate in making appointments.

To guard against this possibility the plan was once more changed. In case the electoral vote for president should not prove decisive, the choice was to go to the House instead of the Senate. But the smaller states were not pushed out of the picture. For in voting for president, the House was to follow the old Confederation rule, with each state, no matter what its size, casting just one vote.

Before the plan, after three long months, was written into the Constitution, one last objection was made. A vice-president, to preside over the Senate, had been the committee's own invention. And Gerry—afraid that the president would be so close to the vice-president that he would bargain and trade with the Senate, instead of standing on his own feet—was "against having any vice-president" at all.

But in later years, he was doubtless glad he was voted down. For Gerry, alone of all the delegates, in time became a vice-president himself.

The election puzzle finally solved, the Convention lost no time over the other provisions dealing with the president. He must be a native-born American. He must be at least thirty-five years old. As well as making important appointments, and holding a veto power over Congress, he was to make foreign treaties with the Senate's consent, and act as commander-in-chief of the army and navy. And, of course, he was to supervise the enforcement of national laws.

The famous "separation of powers," about which so much has since been written, was now complete. The strong new central government was divided into three branches — legislative,

165

executive, and judicial. Each branch was separate from the others. Each had some sort of check on the others. And the most important branch, the legislative, was even divided against itself.

Congress was to make the laws. But all laws must be passed by both halves of Congress—the House, elected by the people for terms of two years, and the more stable Senate, chosen by the state legislatures for overlapping terms of six years.

The president was to check these laws with his veto power. He, not Congress, was also to enforce the laws. And he, in turn, was to be elected, not by Congress, not by the people, not by the state legislatures, but, in most cases, by electors specially picked for the purpose. He was to hold office, not for two years, not for six, but for four. And he could be thrown out of office if the House impeached him, and the Senate, with the chief justice of the Supreme Court presiding, convicted him.

The judges were to apply, interpret, and thus help enforce the laws. Instead of being elected, they were to be appointed by the president, with the consent, not of the democratic House, but of the more aristocratic Senate. They were to serve, not for a term of years, but for life. And

166

they were to hold a final rein on both Congress and the president, in their power to refuse to help carry out any laws or any enforcement activities they might consider unconstitutional.

This separation of powers, with its many checks and balances, was a great deal more than a pretty political theory. It had a definite and extremely practical purpose. And though Madison and a few other delegates, in urging this separation of powers, occasionally quoted the general views of Montesquieu and other political theorists, they knew, and made perfectly clear, what its practical purpose was.

Its purpose was two-fold. In the first place, it was to protect all the people from the tyranny of a president turned dictator or king. The delegates had had enough of King George III.

In the second place, it was to protect, not all, but a part of the people from a type of government the delegates themselves feared even more. That type of government was government by all the people. It was democracy, undiluted, as then practiced in the separate states. It was the kind of democracy that, more than any other single thing, had brought the Convention together, to put a stop to it.

For, that democracy had scant respect for property rights. It soaked the rich with paper

167

money laws, "leveling laws," high taxes on business, and other schemes tending toward a more
equal distribution of wealth. And the delegates,
founding a national government to stop that sort
of stuff in the states, wanted none of it in the
government they were founding.

At one point, it was suggested that only
property owners be allowed to vote in national
elections. Dickinson called this "a necessary
defence against the dangerous influence of those
multitudes without property and without principle, with which our country, like all others, will
in time abound."

The scheme, like that of making members of
Congress be property owners, was dropped as
too hard to put across. Wilson reminded the
delegates that it would be "difficult to form any
uniform rule." And Ellsworth dubbed it a
"tender point," because "the people will not
readily subscribe to the national Constitution if
it should subject them to be disfranchised."

But Madison, at a later date, pointed out
that almost the same result was achieved by the
separation of powers. Going over the notes he
had taken, he wrote that he no longer approved,
as he once had, of property qualifications for
national voters. He no longer thought them
proper or necessary.

He still realized "the danger to the holders of property, if they be undefended against a majority without property." Yet, "the characteristic excellence of the political system of the United States arises from a distribution and organization of its powers, which at the same time that they secure the dependence of the government on the will of the nation, provide better guards than are found in any other popular government against interested combinations of a majority against the rights of a minority."

Thus, the separation of powers softened the strength of real majority rule in order to guard the property interests of less than half the people. For it gave to Senate, president, and judges, all in turn, a separate chance to scuttle any laws the people's House might try to pass.

The structure of the government now was solid and secure. The delegates had finally fitted the last piece into the picture. Their long task would soon be ended.

IX

"ALL THE STATES AY"

C ONTROL of the nation and its affairs had been taken out of the hands of the states and given to the central government. Control of the central government had been kept as far as possible out of the hands of the people as a whole. But it was not enough just to rescue business and trade and property from those who had been treating them unkindly. The commercial affairs of the new nation must also be given a firm helping hand.

One way to lend business a hand would be to repay the money that had been borrowed to carry on the Revolution. The failure of the Confederation to make good on these loans, or on the certificates issued to the soldiers, had been hurting American credit at home and abroad. Payment, even at this late date, would be welcomed by all business-men, as well as by those who held the government papers. By boosting American credit in the eyes of foreign nations, it might lead to investment of foreign money in American business.

So when Morris moved that Congress, by command of the Constitution, "*shall* discharge the debts and fulfill the engagements of the

United States," every state on the list shouted aye.

Yet, would it be fair to pay the whole face value of the government's promises, to men who had bought them for a fraction of that value? Some of these buyers, according to Butler, were nothing but "blood-suckers who have speculated on the distresses of others." And Mason, too, deplored "the pestilent practice of stock-jobbing."

But Mason added that he did "not mean to include those who have bought stock in open market," although he realized "the difficulty of drawing the line." And Gerry rose in defense of the "stock-jobbers," admitting that he held a few of the government papers himself. He was sorry for the soldiers, "these poor and ignorant people," who had sold their pay-certificates cheap. Nevertheless he thought the government debts ought to be paid at face value.

To save argument, the absolute command to Congress was softened. The debts were declared "as valid under this Constitution as under the Confederation." And with this none too gentle hint, the actual payment was left to the discretion of Congress.

An effort was also made to order the new government to take over the debts of the states.

174

For the states, too, had borrowed money to help pay for the Revolution, and these debts, as Rutledge said, "were contracted in the common defence." Moreover, as King pointed out, "the state creditors, an active and formidable party, will otherwise be opposed" to the Constitution.

But Gerry wanted the national funds saved to pay national debts. He thought the states which had done the most to pay off their debts themselves ought not be "saddled with a share of the debts of states which have done the least." So the state debts were not even mentioned in the Constitution.

Instead, in the final list of laws that Congress could pass, the power "to pay the debts" was coupled with the power "to provide for the common defence and general welfare of the United States." Again, the hint was there. "Common defence and general welfare" could refer to the past as well as the future. And under Hamilton's urging, as secretary of the treasury, Congress eventually did pay both the national and the state debts in full.

Yet, if payment of government debts was important to business, even more important was national control of money. Of course, Congress itself had power to coin money and manage the national currency. And of course, so far as the states were concerned, Congress was supreme.

But this was one place where the delegates refused to take any chances. Throughout the Convention, the mere mention of the states' paper money laws never failed to produce the desired effect. It was very much like the effect produced by the mention of communism today. Mercer was indeed a brave man to confess before that assembly that he was a "friend to paper money" himself.

So when it was proposed that the Constitution absolutely forbid the states to coin money, to print money, or to let anything but gold and silver coin be used in payment of debts, there was virtually no discussion.

Gorham wondered for a minute how wise it would be to line up all the paper money addicts against the Constitution. But the other delegates agreed just about unanimously with Sherman that "crushing paper money" for good was a vital necessity. Better, almost, to have no Constitution at all, than one which allowed that evil to continue.

But there were other dodges than the payment of debts in cheap paper money or in goods, by which the states had been letting debtors squirm out of their business obligations. Laws had been passed reducing debts, postponing payment, and sometimes denying there was any further obligation at all. So, although no similar restriction on the national government was considered fitting or proper, the states, like bad boys who could not be trusted, were forbidden to "pass any law impairing the obligation of contracts."

Payment of government debts, and complete control of the currency so that private debts would also be paid in full, were only two of the ways in which the new government was to help business—in which it was to help the people who had loaned and invested money. There was still another way. This was by using its brand-new teeth, its power to tax and to regulate, in behalf of national trade and national industry.

King remarked that of all the purposes for which Congress could make laws, "the chief of them are commerce and revenue." And Wilson —who had earlier put in a word for "the cultivation and improvement of the human mind"— agreed that regulation and taxes, along with war, were apparently "the great objects of the general government." "All of them," he added quietly, "are connected with money."

Yet, if Congress was to help American industry by putting tariffs on foreign goods, if it was to help American business by clearing the

177

way for national trade as well as by clamping down on the squirming debtors, what about the South? For the wealth of the South was not in shops and mills and trading companies. Although some few Southern gentlemen were business investors themselves, the real wealth of the South was in its plantations and its slaves.

So, tariffs and regulations would be no blessing to the South. Both might be directed against the slaves who worked the plantations. Neither would help the Southern states find the foreign markets they needed for their tobacco, their rice, and their indigo.

As Pinckney of South Carolina said, "the power of regulating commerce is a pure concession on the part of the Southern states." And Gorham of Massachusetts went so far as to admit that "the Eastern states have no motive to union but a commercial one." It was therefore only natural that the South should demand protection for its particular brand of property, too.

First of all came the slaves. Even with three-fifths of the slaves counting toward Southern representatives, there was no doubt that the Northern and middle Atlantic states could outvote the Southern in both houses of Congress. There was also no doubt that many citizens north of the Maryland border already resented the

178

whole idea of slavery.

This resentment broke out in the Convention as soon as the far South asked that Congress be forbidden to stop importation of slaves. Gouverneur Morris jumped to his feet to condemn slavery as a "nefarious institution" and "the curse of heaven on the states where it prevails."

"Compare," he cried, "the free regions of the middle states, where a rich and noble cultivation marks the prosperity and happiness of the people, with the misery and poverty which overspread the barren wastes of Virginia, Maryland, and other states having slaves." Bitter with moral indignation, he spoke of "the inhabitant of Georgia and South Carolina who goes to the coast of Africa, and in defiance of the most sacred laws of humanity tears away his fellow creatures from their dearest connections and damns them to the most cruel bondages."

But Rutledge of South Carolina poured the cold water of economics on Northern oratory. "Religion and humanity," he said, "have nothing to do with this question." For, the slave trade and the products of slavery meant business for the shippers. And the shipping trade was centered in the North. "If the Northern states," Rutledge told them, "consult their interest, they will not oppose the increase of

179

slaves which will increase the commodities of which they will become the carriers."

His fellow-statesman Pinckney was more blunt. "South Carolina," he warned, "can never receive the plan if it prohibits the slave trade." Or, he might have added, if it leaves the way open to such prohibition.

But Martin, although from the slave state, Maryland, felt that writing protection of the slave trade into the Constitution would be "inconsistent with the principles of the Revolution and dishonorable to the American character." And Mason, although from Virginia, admitted that "slavery discourages arts and manufactures." A trifle righteously, he pointed out that "Maryland and Virginia have already prohibited the importation of slaves."

Ellsworth of Connecticut could not let Martin and Mason get away with this. He reminded the Convention that "slaves multiply so fast in Virginia and Maryland that it is cheaper to raise than import them." And if the slave trade were stopped, the far Southern states, where the slaves died off fast in the rice swamps, would have to buy more from Virginia and Maryland.

Pinckney took up the same thread. "South Carolina and Georgia," he insisted, "cannot do without slaves. As to Virginia she will gain by

180

rtations. Her slaves will rise
has more than she wants."

vention," chimed in Rutledge,
orth Carolina, South Carolina,
and   will ever agree to the plan, unless
their right to import slaves be untouched, the
expectation is vain. The people of those states
will never be such fools."

The Northern states were not prepared to
fight about it. After all, they had seen to it
that their property was pretty well protected.
As Sherman of Connecticut said, it would be
"better to let the Southern states import slaves,
than to part with them." And Williamson of
North Carolina—a state not yet sure whether it
needed to import slaves or not—drawled that he,
too, thought it "more in favor of humanity, from
a view of all circumstances, to let in South Carolina and Georgia on those terms, than to exclude
them from the Union."

So Congress was forbidden, for twenty years,
to put a stop to the slave trade, and also forbidden, for the same period, to tax the importation of slaves at more than ten dollars a head.
And any amendment to the Constitution, relax-
ing these restrictions, was also forbidden "prior
to the year 1808." The South felt that in
twenty years, the Southern states would have

grown enough to take care of themselves in Congress.

In the meanwhile, one more piece of protection was given to the slave-owners. The non-slave states were ordered to return fugitive slaves to their masters. But the North did not object to this. For the clause was worded to require, as well, the return of run-away white servants to Northern masters.

Yet, the Southern states wanted protection of more than the slaves themselves. Although Southern wealth was built on the slaves, the products of slavery had to be sold to be turned to profits. And the biggest markets for tobacco and other Southern products lay across the Atlantic.

Congress, however, could easily make the exporting business unprofitable, through its power to tax and regulate foreign trade. Moreover, New England and the middle states were not yet so interested in selling their products abroad as in selling them at home. Afraid that these states would try to fill the national treasury with taxes on Southern exports, the South asked that Congress be forbidden to tax exports at all.

"If slaves are to be imported," came the reply from King of Massachusetts, "shall not the exports produced by their labor supply a revenue,

182

the better to enable the general government to defend their masters?" But Mason of Virginia, one eye-brow lifted, hoped that, after all the protection given to business, "the Northern states do not mean to deny the Southern this security."

Madison, however, sided with King. He feared that, if Congress could not tax exports, they would be taxed by the states that shipped them abroad. And this "would be unjust to the states whose produce is exported by their neighbors." Madison therefore argued that, so far as a national tax was concerned, "the Southern states being most in danger and most needing naval protection, should the less complain if the burthen should be somewhat heaviest on them."

But Mercer of Maryland had the answer to this. Instead of the Southern states needing the protection of an American navy, "the reverse is the case. Were it not for promoting the carrying trade of the Northern states, the Southern states could let the trade go into foreign bottoms, where it would not need our protection."

Sherman and Ellsworth of Connecticut saw that, as well as discouraging American shipping, export taxes might eventually "discourage industry." For as time went on, the manufacturing states would want to do more and more exporting themselves. Then too, varying taxes

183

on the different products exported by various sections of the country would, as Ellsworth put it, "engender incurable jealousies."

And even with the North doing its own exporting, Mason was certain the South would be hit the hardest. He foresaw that "a majority when interested will oppress the minority. If we compare the states in this point of view, the eight Northern states have an interest different from the five Southern states; and have in one branch of the legislature 36 votes against 29, and in the other the proportion of 8 against 5."

Again, the North did not protest for long. Its own interests were sufficiently secure. So, largely as a favor to the foreign trade of the South, Congress was forbidden—and is still forbidden by the Constitution—to tax exports bound for foreign shores.

There was, however, another way open for the new government to discriminate against Southern trade. The president, with the consent of the Senate, was to make treaties with foreign nations. Commercial treaties might favor Northern interests, at the expense of the products of Southern plantations.

In order to guard against this, the South asked that no foreign treaty be entered into without the consent of two-thirds of the Senate.

For the South could muster a little more than a third of the Senate vote, if necessary to block a treaty that threatened Southern trade.

Again, as soon as the North objected, it was Mason of Virginia who asked if the Southern states were expected to "deliver themselves bound hand and foot to the Eastern states, and enable them to exclaim, in the words of Cromwell—'the Lord hath delivered them into our hands'." Again, the North gave in. And again, the rule that two-thirds of the Senate must agree to foreign treaties is still, today, a part of the Constitution.

In the meantime, the point that Madison had raised, about state export taxes, had not been forgotten. As a matter of fact, one of the chief obstacles to national trade under the Confederation had been the taxes laid by the separate states on goods shipped in or out across their boundaries.

Like little nations, the states had built their own tariff walls. New York, for instance, taxed cabbages sent in from New Jersey. And so far as exports were concerned, the states with Atlantic ports took peculiar pleasure in taxing the products of other states, when they were shipped from these ports to Europe.

But from now on, the national government was

to regulate foreign and interstate trade, for the good of the country as a whole. State import and export taxes must be stopped, even where they were only meant to encourage local industry. It was therefore proposed that the states be forbidden to levy such taxes without the consent of Congress, and that whenever consent was granted, all money collected be turned over to the national treasury.

Only one or two delegates protested. Clymer of Pennsylvania was one—for Maryland, New Jersey, and Delaware had been shipping their products abroad through the port of Philadelphia. King of Massachusetts was another—for Boston was also a big Atlantic port.

Both men, however, based their protests on the right of the separate states to control and encourage industry within their borders. "If the states," said Clymer, "have such different interests that they cannot be left to regulate their own manufactures without encountering the interests of other states, it is a proof that they are not fit to compose one nation." And, King, too, was afraid the restriction would "too much interfere with the policy of states respecting their manufactures."

But the cry of state rights, for another purpose, had been heard, and answered, before.

Clymer and King got their answer even faster.

Madison, for one, had seen enough of "the mischiefs experienced from the want of a general government over commerce." Wilson and Morris, from Clymer's own state, could not accept Clymer's argument. These men made it clear that, from now on, state control of state industry must take a back seat wherever it hindered national control of national trade. And the Convention voted with them.

The commercial interests of the North, the South, and the nation as a whole were now safe in the hands of the national government. A few more points, some important, some minor, and the Constitution would be complete.

Two clauses were written in to keep the large states from taking unfair advantage of the small ones. Congress, in taxing and regulating trade, was forbidden to favor the ports of one state over those of another. And no state was to be permitted to swallow up a neighboring state without the neighboring state's consent.

One of the minor points was the rule that Congress should meet every year on the first Monday in December. Madison said May would be better than December "because the latter will require the travelling to and from the seat of government in the most inconvenient seasons of the

187

year"—and winter travel was indeed "inconvenient" in 1787. But December was chosen because farmers and plantation-owners in Congress would find it even more inconvenient to leave their crops in May.

Perhaps with Benedict Arnold in mind, the delegates spent considerable time defining the crime of treason. And they guaranteed that no man should be convicted of treason except on the word of at least two witnesses, or else on his own confession in court.

This last provision, and four others, were meant to protect the people against criminal punishment by high-handed government action. One of the others forbade Congress to pass any "bills of attainder"—laws in which Congress itself picked out certain individuals and sentenced them directly to jail or to death. Congress was also forbidden to pass any "ex post facto laws"—laws punishing people for things they had done before the laws were passed. A third provision guaranteed a jury trial to every man arrested on a criminal charge. And a fourth promised that, except when "the public safety" was in danger, any man who was put to prison without a fair trial could use a "writ of habeas corpus" to get himself out of jail.

But the delegates did not put into the Constitution a real "bill of rights," to guarantee to every man such personal liberties as freedom of speech, freedom of the press, and freedom to meet peacefully with other men and protest against the government. Nor was this merely a slip on the part of the members.

For Mason asked that a bill of rights be included. "It will give great quiet to the people," he said. It could be "prepared in a few hours." And when Sherman answered that the bills of rights in the state constitutions were enough, Mason reminded him that "the laws of the United States are to be paramount to the state bills of rights."

Perhaps the Convention was in too great a hurry to get home. A vote was called as to whether a committee should draw up a bill of rights. And every state on the floor voted no.

Within a few months, the delegates were to learn they had made a mistake in leaving a bill of rights out of the Constitution. They did not, however, make the mistake of keeping the people from writing one in. For they did, of course, provide for future amendments.

And it was Mason who, in the early weeks of the Convention, explained why a method of changing the Constitution must be contained in the document itself. Since changes would be

189

wanted, he said, "it will be better to provide for them in an easy, regular, and constitutional way than to trust to chance and violence."

The territory of the nation, too, as well as its form of government, would need room for change and growth. So provision was made for admitting new states to the Union. And, to please the sections that were later to become Maine, Vermont, and Kentucky, a way was left open for forming new states out of chunks of old ones.

Then, the part of the Constitution that was, in 1787, perhaps the most important of all was put at its very end. It had to do with the way in which the Constitution itself was to be adopted. And this, as the Convention knew, was a very delicate question.

For the members, after all, were sent to Philadelphia under orders. Those orders were to revise the Articles of Confederation, and nothing more. One of the rules of the Articles was that they could never be changed without the consent of the legislatures of all the thirteen states.

It was all very well for the delegates, in closed and secret meeting, to toss their orders lightly aside. It was all very well to quiet the small states' suddenly acquired "scruples" with the promise of equal votes in the new Senate. But when news got out to the people of what the Convention had done, when the states discovered the Confederation had been entirely scrapped, when it came to getting the Constitution ratified, there might be a different story.

Yet, the delegates were bold and practical men. They had met to accomplish a bold and practical purpose. They were going to let neither qualms nor technicalities stand in their way.

The state legislatures, the delegates knew, would never sign away their own powers, by approving a document specially designed to take those powers from them. And even if, by some miracle, the legislatures should accept the new government, they would consider themselves supreme over that government, from the very fact that they had created it.

But if the Constitution were submitted to the people, it would stand a better chance of being accepted. One group of the people, at least, would be heartily for it. Moreover, if the people themselves should accept it, the states could no longer claim that they were supreme.

So the delegates decided the Constitution should be submitted, not to the legislatures, but instead to conventions elected by the people.

191

And they also decided that acceptance by nine, not all, of the thirteen conventions should put the Constitution into effect. For they knew that, no matter who did the accepting, they started with Rhode Island—and maybe New York, and maybe Maryland, and maybe others, against them.

* * *

It was now early September. The delegates chose a committee "of style" to put the finishing touches to the Constitution. On that committee were Madison, Hamilton, Gouverneur Morris, Johnson and King.

But the actual phrasing of the document was largely the work of one man. That man was Gouverneur Morris. And the body of the Constitution still stands in the words that Morris gave it.

By the time the final draft was ready, some of the delegates had left Philadelphia. Only forty-two stayed to the end. But in those forty-two was included at least one man from every state that had taken a part in the Convention.

For a day or two after the draft was presented, there was some discussion. A few small changes were made. Then, on Saturday, September 15, it came time for the most important vote of the whole four months.

192

As Madison jotted it briefly down: "On the question to agree to the Constitution—All the states ay." The following Monday, the Convention met for the last time. On that day, Washington made his only speech since he had taken the presiding chair. He supported Gorham's motion to make one final change, so that each state could have a congressman for every 30,000, instead of for every 40,000 citizens. His word was enough to make the vote unanimous.

It was on the last day too, that Wilson got up to read for Franklin a speech that the old gentleman had prepared. A few of the members had said they were not going to sign the Constitution. Franklin did not approve of every point in the document, but he was "astonished" to find it "approaching so near to perfection as it does." Moreover, "the older I grow, the more apt I am to doubt my own judgment, and to pay more respect to the judgment of others." So he, for one, was going to sign it gladly.

At the end, of the forty-two delegates left, only three refused to sign. Mason was one. He had said, some days earlier, that "I would sooner chop off my right hand than put it to the Constitution as it now stands." He had not since changed his mind.

Gerry was another. He took some offense at Franklin's comments which he felt were directed at him. But he was afraid those people of Massachusetts who were "devoted to democracy, the worst, I think, of all political evils," would start a civil war in opposition to the Constitution.

The third who refused to sign was Randolph —he who had presented the original plan when the Convention opened. He apologized to all, including Franklin, for feeling bound to follow his conscience. And he realized that, "in refusing to sign the Constitution, I take a step which may be the most awful of my life."

Then, Franklin made his famous remark about the sun that was painted at the back of the president's chair. "Painters," he said, "have found it difficult to distinguish in their art a rising from a setting sun. I have often and often in the course of the session, and the vicissitudes of my hopes and fears as to its issue, looked at that behind the president without being able to tell whether it was rising or setting. But now at length I have the happiness to know that it is a rising and not a setting sun."

And while he was talking, the last few of the thirty-nine faithful members were putting their names at the end of the words which begin: "We the People of the United States—"

194

X

CLOSER AND CLOSER TO DEMOCRACY

ELBRIDGE GERRY was not quite right. The Constitution, finished at last and at last made public, did not touch off a civil war. But it did bring to a head one of the bitterest political battles the nation has ever known.

The real fight between central control of national affairs and local self-government, between national power and state power, between property rights and personal liberty, did not come on the floor of the Convention. It came afterward, over the business of choosing state conventions to accept or turn down the Constitution. And it came on the floor of those conventions, meeting to decide whether they wanted the plan that the founding fathers offered them.

Lined up on one side were the business-men and the manufacturers, the men with money invested and money to invest. With them were most of the big plantation-owners of the South, who saw nothing to lose in the new government, and perhaps something to gain.

These were the men "of wealth and substance." They believed, as did the framers themselves, in a strong central government. They approved of keeping control of that gov-

197

ernment away from the mass of the people. In
their own interests—and, to their minds, in the
interest of the nation—they wanted that government to protect property, trade, and business,
even at the expense of real democracy.

Fighting against these men, and against the
Constitution, were the poor, the small farmers,
the men who worked with their hands. They
were the men who owed money and found money
hard to earn. They were the men who then
controlled most of the state legislatures, and
helped themselves with paper money and other
"leveling laws."

Among them were many patriots of the Revolution. Patrick Henry by no means stood alone.
And they saw in the Constitution exactly what
he had suspected—a threat to the liberty so hard-
won and so recently won from England. They
no more wanted to go ahead under such a Constitution than they wanted to go back to King
George III.

Lined up with them were some few men of
high position who believed whole-heartedly in democracy—men who believed, as most of the
framers did not believe, that the people could
be trusted to govern themselves.

It was not considered heresy, in 1787, to call
the Constitution bad names. Men who favored

ratification were denounced as un-American just as often as the men who fought against it. Each group battled desperately for the cause it was defending, and hurled its scorn at defenders of the other cause.

All the weapons of propaganda were used on both sides. Pamphlets were printed. Speeches were made. The newspapers of the day were flooded with pieces that either praised or damned the Constitution.

A small but important part of that propaganda, since become famous, was a series of papers written by three men. The three men were Madison, Hamilton, and John Jay, who was soon to be made the Supreme Court's first chief justice. The papers they wrote are known as the Federalist papers.

The Federalist papers, beautifully worded and most persuasively argued, put the case for the Constitution in its best light. And perhaps because they make pleasant reading, or perhaps for other reasons, they are commonly used today to discover the intent of the founding fathers. History teachers and Supreme Court members, alike, turn to the Federalist papers to explain what the Constitution means, and why.

It is true that there runs through the Federalist papers the thread of the arguments used on the floor of the Constitutional Convention. Madison, Hamilton, and Jay were appealing especially to men of affairs, to men of the type of the delegates themselves. And yet, they could not afford to go too far.

In the Federalist papers, there was less plain talk of the horrors of democracy. The people were not so bluntly described as fools. Protection of property was to be one of the objects of the government, not its only nor its primary object.

There was more stress laid on the public welfare of the nation as a whole, and less on the commercial interests of some of its citizens. There was more talk of helping the states to solve their separate problems, and less of keeping them well under thumb. In other words, things that were spoken out clear and bold, in the Convention, were blurred and toned down in defense of what the Convention had done.

For, the Federalist papers, after all, were published. The proceedings of the Convention had been secret. The Convention had met to draw up a Constitution, which the Federalist papers were later designed to sell. And so far as what the framers intended, and why, is ever concerned, the Federalist papers are the campaign speeches of the party's ablest orators.

200

The debates are the record of the closed meeting that mapped the campaign plans.

Yet, it took more than the smooth appeals of Madison, Hamilton, and Jay to sell the Constitution to the people. Martin of Maryland— just before he quit the Convention in disgust when it was almost over—had warned the delegates they would have to work fast to put their plan across. He was 'sure the people would not take long to catch on to what the framers really wanted. "They will not," he said, "ratify it unless hurried into it by surprize."

So the delegates and those who sided with them did work fast. They were better organized, from the start, than their opponents. They saw to it that, in most states, the popular elections, to choose men to sit in the state conventions, were called with the greatest possible speed.

On at least one occasion, friends of the Constitution resorted to physical force. That was in Pennsylvania, where most of the members of the legislature itself were in favor of ratification, and therefore wanted to set the election at an early date.

Their opponents in the legislature walked out of the session, to take time to talk things over. They left less than a quorum on the floor. Be-

201

fore they had a chance to get together, they were unceremoniously dragged from their homes and back to their seats. Immediately, a vote was taken. The popular election was set in the near future.

Speed such as this did prove effective. News of any sort traveled slowly in those days, especially to the backwoods sections. Many of the farmers away from the sea-coast, the real rugged individualists of their time, did not know enough about what was going on to bother to go to the polls. Most of them would doubtless have voted against the Constitution.

Thus, the battle over ratification, fiercely as it was waged, was pretty well confined to narrow quarters. In the actual elections themselves throughout the thirteen states, only one quarter of the male, white citizens over twenty-one—in other words, barely a hundred and fifty thousand men—so much as cast their votes for delegates to the state conventions.

The haste with which the elections were called, and the resulting ignorance of many people of the importance of what was happening, helped to cut down the popular vote. But there were other reasons. One was the fact that most of the states put property qualifications on their voters.

These qualifications were not of the kind that many of the Convention delegates had wanted to write into the Constitution. For the most part, they only required that every voter own a piece of land. Thus, practically all the small farmers were entitled to vote, no matter how deeply they might be in debt. But a large part of them never got around to helping choose men to decide on the Constitution. And most of the growing group of workers in shops and mills were not allowed to vote at all.

Nevertheless, after the elections were over, the fight had to be carried into the state conventions. In spite of the hasty selection of members, in spite of propaganda of every sort, in spite of the great names signed to the document, the actual voters in many states were far from convinced that they wanted the Constitution.

In New York, New Hampshire, and Massachusetts, for instance, most of the popular votes were cast for men who were against the Constitution at the time those votes were cast. But in all three states, political maneuvers were used in the conventions to swing enough of the members over to the ratification side.

It was on December 7, less than three months after the Constitution was made public, that little

203

Delaware became the first state to ratify. Five days later, Pennsylvania followed suit. Then, in order, came New Jersey, Georgia, Connecticut, Massachusetts, Maryland, and South Carolina.

And on June 21, 1788, New Hampshire became the ninth state to agree to the Constitution. Just one year and two days after the Philadelphia Convention had voted to scrap the Confederation and build a new form of government, the founding fathers had put across that momentous decision. The Constitution, by its own terms, could now go into effect.

After this, it did not take long for Virginia, and then New York, to come around. But North Carolina held out until late in the following year. And rebel Rhode Island refused to join till the summer of 1790, a few months before Vermont became the fourteenth state in the Union.

Yet, propaganda and political maneuvers, speed and occasional drastic measures, had not in themselves been enough to turn the tide. The friends of the Constitution, in their battle to get it accepted, had also promised to change and soften it. And convention members in doubtful states had voted for ratification in exchange for, and reliance on, these promises.

Most of the promises called for the immediate addition of a real bill of rights. This, of course, could be done by amendment. And many who thought the original document a threat to the people's liberties were only appeased by assurance that those liberties would soon be guaranteed.

Thomas Jefferson, over in France, had been shocked to hear that a bill of rights was not included. He helped lead the movement to write one in. And he was later won over to support the Constitution by the very fact that it provided a way for the people themselves to amend it.

So, the first Congress, in 1789, submitted a bill of rights to the nation. And the first ten amendments to the Constitution have been known as the Bill of Rights ever since.

These ten amendments, this Bill of Rights, can hardly be considered a part of the work of the founding fathers. True, Madison presented them in the House of Representatives. And his fellow delegates did not oppose them now.

But this was more than two years after the Philadelphia Convention had voted down a bill of rights, unanimously. And in those two years, the framers had learned that what was not so important to them was most important to the people of the United States. For the Bill of Rights was part of the price the framers had to pay to get the people to ratify their Constitution.

So far as the people's liberties were concerned, the first amendment was the most important of all. In one sentence, it guaranteed more to the ordinary citizen than did the whole seven articles of the original Constitution. For it forbade Congress to interfere with freedom of religion, freedom of speech, freedom of the press, or freedom of the people to get together peacefully and protest against the government.

The second amendment, since ringed around with local police restrictions, gave every citizen the right to own and carry a gun. The third, after sad experiences with British colonial troops, protected the people from being forced to put up soldiers in their homes. And under the fourth amendment, even citizens suspected of crime were guarded against having their homes broken into, their clothes searched, or their belongings taken without a properly issued search warrant.

The fifth amendment was divided into four parts. Its first part guaranteed every man suspected of serious crime the right to have a grand jury consider the charges against him, before the case could even be taken to court. The second part protected every man from being tried again for a crime of which he had once been declared innocent. The fourth part forbade the government to take over private property without paying for it.

The third part of the fifth amendment was later destined to have a strange history. And the second half of that third part was to become more important to lawyers—except to criminal lawyers, for whose use it was written—than all the rest of the Bill of Rights put together. Yet, the third part of the fifth amendment, taken as a whole, dealt, as did the first two parts, with the handling of criminal cases. It provided, and it still reads, that no person "shall be compelled in any criminal case to be a witness against himself, nor be deprived of life, liberty, or property, without due process of law."

The sixth amendment continued to deal with criminal matters. It enlarged the bare right to a jury trial, as granted by the original Constitution, by insisting that the trial be "speedy" and "public" and before an "impartial" jury. And it also promised the man on trial the right to know what he was being tried for, the right to hear the evidence against him, the right to produce his own evidence, and the right to have a lawyer defend him.

The seventh amendment extended the right to a jury trial from criminal cases to all important law suits of any kind. The eighth protected men under arrest from having to pay "excessive bail;" and protected men convicted of crime from "excessive fines" and from "cruel and unusual punishments."

Then, with so many personal rights and liberties definitely named, in black and white, in the first eight amendments, the ninth provided a much more general safe-guard. It made clear that the listing of these rights and liberties did not mean that others, left off the list, could therefore be taken from the people.

At the end of the Bill of Rights came the tenth amendment. As a sort of sop to the states, it promised that any powers not given to the national government by the Constitution were to be "reserved to the states respectively, or to the people." This, of course, took nothing away from the powers which had been given to the national government. And for that reason, it bothered the friends of a strong central government no more than it had bothered them to strike the word "national" out of the document. They were satisfied that the powers were already

208

there.

But the eleventh amendment, adopted a few years after the Bill of Rights, made a real, although small, concession to the states. It forbade the national courts to hear any law suit brought against a state by a citizen.

And just after the turn of the century, the Constitution had to be amended again. In spite of the care the framers had used to outline the complicated way that presidents were to be elected, a flaw was discovered. For, in the election of 1800, with electors casting two votes apiece, Thomas Jefferson and Aaron Burr were tied for president.

The two men had run on the same ticket. But the electors, merely casting two ballots, had not been able to say that their presidential choice was Jefferson. And the House of Representatives came close to picking Burr, who was meant to be the vice-presidential candidate.

So the twelfth amendment changed the rule under which each elector voted twice and the man with the second largest vote became vice-president. It provided, instead, that each elector should cast one vote for president, and then cast one for vice-president separately.

For sixty years, then, until just after the end of the Civil War, no other changes were made in the Constitution. But every one of the nine amendments added since, with one exception, has made the national government more nearly of the people, by the people, and for the people.

The one exception, of course, was the eighteenth amendment, in 1919,—the noble experiment that even narrowed the meaning of the word "prohibition." And when the people, fourteen years later, repealed that amendment with the twenty-first, they showed that they themselves could realize, and correct, their own mistakes.

Like the first ten amendments, the thirteenth, fourteenth, and fifteenth are usually lumped together. As the Bill of Rights was intended to guard the hard-won liberties of all the people, so these three amendments were meant to protect the equally hard-won liberties of the recent slaves. And again, the movement in behalf of those liberties was led by a man who had greater faith in democracy than did the founding fathers.

Abraham Lincoln had already freed the slaves by proclamation when the first of the three amendments was adopted. He did not even live to see written into the Constitution the words that forever abolished slavery in the United States. For he was shot in April, 1865, eight months before the thirteenth amendment became part of the law of the land.

The fourteenth, longest of all the amendments, came three years later. Its first and most important part was also meant to protect the rights of the negroes. Even though they were no longer slaves, they still were not being treated as citizens.

So the first part of this amendment made clear that every person born or naturalized in the United States was a citizen of the nation and of his home state. It then forbade the states to pass any law cutting down the rights of any citizen. And it forbade the states to "deprive any person of life, liberty, or property without due process of law," or to take from any person "the equal protection of the laws."

The rest of the fourteenth amendment fitted the Constitution to the aftermaths of the Civil War. It struck out the old compromise whereby three-fifths of the Southern slaves counted toward seats in the House of Representatives. And to further guard the slaves, it threatened to reduce the number of congressmen allowed any state that tried to keep some of its citizens from voting.

The amendment also barred from national office every man who had once taken oath to support the Constitution and had then helped

211

the Confederate cause. It disowned completely the Confederate debt. And it outlawed all Southern claims for money to pay for slaves or other personal property lost in the War.

Yet, even the threat of taking congressmen away from any state which kept negroes from voting was not enough. So in 1870, the fifteenth amendment flatly ordered both the nation and the states never to deny any citizen the right to vote "on account of race, color, or previous condition of servitude."

It was not until half a century later that another amendment, the nineteenth, extended much further the right of all the people to run their own government. For it was in 1920 that the long fight for women's suffrage was crowned with success. And since then, every American citizen has been entitled to vote, regardless of race, color, or sex.

In between came the sixteenth amendment, allowing an income tax. The Supreme Court had first declared such a tax unconstitutional. Certainly it might, among other things, be considered one of the "leveling laws" the framers had tried so hard to prevent. But the people decided that, Supreme Court or no Supreme Court, a larger share of the cost of government should be paid by men and companies who could best afford to pay it. And in 1913, they wrote that decision into the Constitution.

Even the twentieth amendment, adopted in 1933, brought the national government closer to the will of the people. It not only let Congress and the president take office a shorter time after election day—for election returns and elected candidates travel faster today than they could in 1787. It also got rid of the "lame duck" Congresses. For as well as moving inaugurations ahead to January, it ruled that Congress should meet in January instead of December. And it thus prevented any members of Congress, not re-elected by the people, from continuing to take a part in making the nation's laws.

But most important of all twenty-one amendments, in bringing the government itself closer to the people, was the seventeenth. That amendment, more than any other, went directly against the desires of the founding fathers. For it took election of senators away from the state legislatures and gave the election straight to the people themselves.

More than twenty years were needed to put that amendment across. Time and again, the House would bring up the idea. Time and again, the Senate would turn it down. But popular pressure finally forced the Senate to give in. And since 1913, both houses of Congress instead of only one have been directly responsible to the people.

Thus, eight of the nine amendments in the last hundred years have brought the nation closer to popular government. Like the first ten amendments, the Bill of Rights, they have tended to advance the interests of ordinary citizens.

The thirteenth, fourteenth, and fifteenth protected the rights of the negroes. The sixteenth permitted an income tax. The seventeenth let the people elect the Senate. The eighteenth, prohibiting liquor, was soon repealed by the twenty-first. The nineteenth gave women the right to vote. And the twentieth prevented members of Congress, once ousted by the people, from having a hand in making the people's laws.

There is, moreover, another amendment to the Constitution that nowhere appears on the face of the document. It might well be called the unwritten amendment. And it too brings the very form of the government closer to the people themselves.

The unwritten amendment is the way the president is elected. A citizen goes into a booth and marks one cross or pulls one lever opposite the name of a candidate. Often he does not even know that technically, under the Constitution, he

214

is not voting for president at all. He is voting for electors who are later to choose the president. And the names of the electors who have promised to vote for a candidate are bunched together in small type after that candidate's name.

For, presidential electors do not make a free choice today. They themselves are chosen beforehand just to satisfy the formal requirement of the Constitution. And not one voter in ten thousand knows or cares who those electors are.

Yet back in 1787, the men who wrote the Constitution refused to trust the people to elect the president. And that mistrust still leaves its mark in the fact that presidential votes are counted by states. For instance, a margin of one lone popular vote, in New York, could throw forty-seven electoral votes to one man. A unanimous popular vote for the same man in the same state could give him no more. So it still is possible, though not very likely, that a candidate for president might get more popular votes than his opponent and yet not win the election.

Nevertheless, today, it is the people who in fact elect the president. And today, of the three great branches of government—legislative, executive, and judicial—only one is not directly responsible to the people. But, as the framers

215

planned things, the people were to choose only one-half of one of those three branches.

Thus, slowly but surely through the years, the American people have broken away from the form of government originally meant for them. They have carved their own initials all over the intent of the fifty-five founding fathers. From the first amendment to the twenty-first—and even without amendment—they have bent and twisted the Constitution closer and closer to democracy.

*Five amendments have become law since 55 MEN first appeared in 1936. Two of the articles detail the length of a president's term and presidential succession; three amendments focus on voting privileges.

The twenty-second amendment limits a president's time in office to two terms, and it defines the term of a person who fulfills an uncompleted presidency. The article reflects concern over Franklin Roosevelt's unprecedented four elections to the presidency.

The twenty-fifth amendment answers a vital question raised after the illness of Dwight Eisenhower and the assassination of John Kennedy: "What happens when the president cannot fulfill his duties?"

The amendment's first section establishes that the vice president becomes commander in chief upon the president's death or resignation, and the second section describes how the vacant vice presidency will be filled. Section 3 outlines action taken when the president notifies Congress he cannot fulfill his duties. The final, lengthy section describes the transfer of powers when others in government determine the president cannot carry out his work.

Articles 23, 24, and 26 refine various voting rights. In 1961, article twenty-three restored to the District of Columbia its voice in presidential elections with provisions for electoral representatives. The district had been without such representation since 1800.

Article twenty-four abolished the poll tax, which was still required by five states when the amendment was adopted in 1964.

In 1971, the twenty-sixth amendment lowered the voting age to 18. This was largely a response to young people's activism over the Vietnam War and their demands for the right to vote.

XI

WHAT WOULD THEY THINK TODAY?

THERE are airplanes and railroads and four-lane concrete highways, these days. Men no longer travel on horse or by stage-coach, and propellors turned by huge engines have taken the place of the wind in the sails of ships. From Boston to the other side of the continent is a faster journey than was the journey from Boston—or from Charleston—to Philadelphia, a long hundred and fifty years ago.

But still the Constitution, as written in 1787 and twenty-one times amended, is the supreme law of the land.* And still men ask—and politicians often purport to answer—what the founding fathers intended and what they would think today.

Perhaps, with Nathaniel Gorham, they never dreamed the thing they were building would stand so long. "Can it be supposed," asked Gorham, at one point in the Convention, "that this vast country including the Western territory will 150 years hence remain one nation?"

Or perhaps they would—as Thomas Jefferson thought they would—consider it silly for folk to bother, in years to come, with what they once had intended.

219

*The Constitution is now twenty-six times amended.

"Some men," wrote Jefferson, in 1816, "look at constitutions with sanctimonious reverence, and deem them like the Ark of the Covenant—too sacred to be touched. They ascribe to the men of the preceding age a wisdom more than human, and suppose what they did to be beyond amendment. I knew that age well; I belonged to it, and labored with it. It deserved well of its country. It was very like the present, but without the experience of the present; and forty years of experience in government is worth a century of book reading; and this they would say themselves were they to rise from the dead."

No, the men who wrote the Constitution were no fools. They knew that, not the Constitution, but the men who held office under it would really determine the course of the nation's destiny. That was why they wanted only the "right kind" of men to hold most of the offices. That was why they tried to restrict, so far as they could with words, the things that the "wrong kind" of men might try to do.

And the cleverest and most effective restriction they used was the separation of national powers. It was the splitting up of the government into three different branches, each with some sort of check on the others, and the splitting up of Congress, the most important branch, into

220

two separate branches of its own.

They did not know in 1787 that, before long, the people would be electing the president. They did not know that, well over a century later, the people would be electing the Senate too. They could not know that, by 1936, only the Supreme Court would be left to check the people's "leveling laws."

Had they guessed all this, they would still have known it would not be the words they put on paper that counted, when it came down to the actual checking of laws. It would be the men who used those words, and the way they used them. And this would be every bit as true when the men who used the written words were Supreme Court judges, interpreting the Constitution.

Some people today have a strange notion. They think that all the Supreme Court ever does or has to do, in order to tell if a law is unconstitutional, is just to look for the answer, written down in black and white, somewhere in the words of the Constitution. The notion persists in spite of the fact that often and often again the nine judges themselves can not agree. It persists in spite of the famous remark of the man who is now the Court's chief justice—and few have put the truth so plainly as did Charles

Evans Hughes—"We are under a Constitution, but the Constitution is what the judges say it is."

Some lawyers pretend this is not the truth. Some professional patriots call it heresy. But the framers, were they alive today, would know with Chief Justice Hughes that the Constitution is what the judges say it is, every time.

There is no better example of this than what the judges have done with the second half of the third part of the fifth amendment. That little piece of the Constitution says no person "shall be deprived of life, liberty, or property, without due process of law." And in 1789, the word "process" was commonly understood as a substitute for another word—"procedure." And being deprived of life, liberty, or property without due process of law meant being hanged, jailed, or fined without a proper trial.

But the Supreme Court has since given the words "due process of law" a meaning entirely different. And most lawyers no longer think of criminal trials at all when they quote that little piece of the fifth amendment. Most lawyers have just about forgotten the fifth amendment was once a part of the people's Bill of Rights.

For the Court has used the amendment's words to declare unconstitutional laws passed by House and Senate and signed by the president, laws having nothing whatever to do with procedure in criminal trials, laws regulating or taxing business and trade. And the Court has given this reason for calling such laws unconstitutional:—that certain owners of property, sometimes men and sometimes companies, would be deprived of property without due process of law, by no other thing than the very laws themselves.

Perhaps, in so using the fifth amendment, the Court has read its words in a way that might have pleased the founding fathers. And yet, it has traveled a long distance away from what was intended by the men who wanted those words in the Constitution.

Moreover, the Court has used the same words in exactly the same way, where they show up again in the fourteenth amendment. For the fifth amendment was meant to protect the people's personal liberties, only against the national government. And part of the fourteenth amendment reads: "nor shall any state deprive any person of life, liberty, or property, without due process of law."

It is true that the Court, under this amendment, has guarded such personal rights as freedom of speech and the right to a fair trial. It

223

has kept the states from enforcing state laws
that seemed to threaten those rights, and from
otherwise interfering with personal liberties.
But again, the Court has used this amendment
many times more often to protect the property
rights of property owners—to declare unconstitutional state laws that taxed or regulated
men of affairs and business corporations.

So many times has this been done that a
strange result has occurred. A state today can
scarcely pass a law that taxes or regulates business corporations or business-men, without being
forced immediately to defend that law in court
against a cry that the fourteenth amendment has
been violated.

It was to spank the rest of the Court for encouraging such cries that Justice Holmes wrote
many of his famous dissents. And in one of the
last of those dissents, he did not even soften his
blows in telling the Court exactly what it was
doing.

"I have not," wrote Holmes, "yet adequately
expressed the more than anxiety that I feel at
the ever increasing scope given to the Fourteenth Amendment in cutting down what I believe to be the constitutional rights of the states.
As the decisions now stand I see hardly any
limit but the sky to the invalidating of those

224

rights if they happen to strike a majority of this Court as for any reason undesirable. I cannot believe that the Amendment was intended to give us carte blanche to embody our economic or moral beliefs in its prohibitions. - - Of course the words 'due process of law' if taken in their literal meaning have no application to this case; - - we should be slow to construe the clause in the Fourteenth Amendment as committing to the Court, with no guide but the Court's own discretion, the validity of whatever laws the States may pass."

For the Court, as no one knew better than Holmes, has turned a few of the words of the fourteenth amendment into a powerful weapon. It has made of those words an excuse to veto any and all state laws that most of the men on the Court do not approve. It has taken upon itself a right that the framers once refused to give to another branch of the national government.

There is, however, a different excuse the Court might use instead, to stop the states from meddling with trade and business. It does not have to change the meaning of "due process of law." It could go all the way back to the founding fathers.

For in 1787, state interference with trade and

225

business was not of the kind that it often is to-day. Such interference amounted mostly to paper money laws, to laws reducing the value of private debts, to other laws making it easier for men who had borrowed money at the cost of men who had money loaned or invested. The only taxes that really left their mark on national trade were the import and export taxes at state borders—the taxes that Pennsylvania put on goods being shipped abroad, that New York put on cabbages crossing the Jersey line.

And the founding fathers forbade all interference of this sort in definite words when they wrote the Constitution. Wherever their own experience showed them a threat to national business or an obstacle in the road of national trade, they ordered the states to quit such threats, to lower all such obstacles, and to clear the track for the nation's commercial affairs.

Moreover the framers, as well as tying the hands of the separate states, gave control of national affairs to the national government. They gave to Congress the right to tax and regulate national trade in any fashion found "necessary and proper."

And so the Supreme Court does not have to resort to the fourteenth amendment to veto state laws affecting national affairs. It could say, instead, that such affairs are the proper concern of Congress and are therefore none of the business of the states.

But the Court, except in extreme cases, does not like to talk like this. When it has to choose between letting the states or the nation control commercial affairs, it seems to prefer to leave control with the states. And this may be why, when it does not approve certain kinds of state control, it vetoes state laws with the words of the fourteenth amendment.

The Court, for instance, has said that only the states can regulate the nation's farms and factories and mines. That is why the N.R.A. and the A.A.A. and other laws have been called unconstitutional by the Court. The Court did not find in black and white in the words of the Constitution the statement that any or all these laws were bad. But it used the words that it did find, in the way it wanted to use them— which is just what the founding fathers knew would happen.

Yet, when it comes down to picking either the nation or the states, to tax and regulate the nation's affairs, the Court is far more anxious today to preserve state rights and flatter state pride than the founding fathers ever would have dreamed. For the founding fathers meant the

227

Court to do just the opposite thing. They meant it to guard the rights and powers of the new-born national government against the cantankerous states and the men who ran them. And this, as a matter of fact, is what the Court once used to do, under men like Justice Marshall, more than a century ago.

Perhaps one of the reasons why the Court has changed its tune is the size to which the nation itself has grown. A country which, at its birth, contained well under four million people is now the home of a hundred and twenty-five million. Where thirteen states were then strung out along the Atlantic seaboard, now forty-eight reach clear across from Atlantic to Pacific, from the Great Lakes to the Gulf and the Rio Grande.*

So large has the nation grown that Congress, the president, and the Cabinet can no longer take care of the nation's laws, by themselves. They have had to set up a lot of special commissions and boards and bureaus, to help them look after the details of running the government. Examples of these are the Interstate Commerce Commission, the Patent Office, the R.F.C., the Bureau of Immigration, the Federal Trade Commission—and also the N.R.A. and the A.A.A., before the Supreme Court called them unconstitutional.

228

---

*In 1985, the United States population was 236.1 million. Alaska and Hawaii round out the number of states to 50, stretching U.S. borders even farther into the Pacific and north to the Arctic Ocean.

It has been the setting up of commissions and boards and bureaus like these that has raised the frequent cry of "bureaucracy!" And the Court, sometimes by its own admission and maybe on other occasions, has heeded this cry in making important decisions. The Court, for instance, said one of the reasons the N.R.A. was bad was that it handed to another group of men the power to help with a law which—though Congress had no right to pass it at all—Congress should have handled all by itself.

Yet, does the Court or anyone else have to worry about bureaucracy while the form of the government stands as it stands today? Is not a fear of bureaucracy, under the present Constitution, a lack of faith in democracy instead?

For no commission or board or bureau can go to work in any field except to help with a law that Congress has passed. No man can hold a job on any commission or board or bureau without the approval of Congress or the president. And today, both houses of Congress, and the president as well, are elected by, and responsible to, the people.

So perhaps the cry of "bureaucracy!" does not mean a fear of bureaucracy at all. Perhaps it means something else.

For almost every commission and board and

bureau is created to help with a certain definite kind of law. That kind of law is the kind that regulates property, trade, or business—that controls the property rights of property owners. And it may just be that the cry of "bureaucracy!" is not really directed at the commissions and boards and bureaus themselves, but against the very kind of law that these commissions and such are almost always created to help enforce.

There is, moreover, a reason why so many laws are passed that regulate business, property, and trade. The nation has not only grown in size since 1787. It has also grown a lot closer to democracy.

And the founding fathers, were they all of a sudden to come to life, would find themselves in a strange position indeed. They would find the powers they once put in the hands of the national government, to protect the property rights of men of affairs, being used in exactly the opposite way—being used to limit those property rights in the interest of a majority of the people.

They would find very little remaining of their separation of powers, with its many checks to guard against popular laws. They would find just one of their three main branches of government removed from the people, instead of two and a half as once they planned.

They would find the Supreme Court left alone to check the "leveling laws" of the nation, as well as those of the states. They would find it single-handed fighting the taxes and regulations imposed, by law, on business and business-men.

They would even see the Court defend the rights of the separate states against the power of the national government. They would see it prefer to give to the states the control of national affairs that they themselves did not want the states to have. And perhaps the founding fathers would approve.

For the nation has grown smaller as it has grown larger. There are airplanes and railroads and four-lane concrete highways now. And almost all of the nation's business and industry and trade is carried on, on a national scale.

State borders were something worth fighting about, in 1787. Just how much do they mean today?

To the criminal, a state border may mean, for a time, escape. To the state politician, it means a livelihood. To the man of affairs, it means the nuisance of filling out forms and paying taxes to a dozen different little governments. And

231

yet, to the average man, a state border means only a line on a map, or a white sign-post along the side of the road.

To business and business-men, however, state borders do mean something more than the nuisance of paying taxes and filling out forms. As a matter of fact, state borders are often a blessing. For they mean that a business carried on from one state to another, as almost all business is carried on today, can not be controlled or regulated by any state alone, nor, effectively, by all the states together.

Today, a company may have its factories in fifteen different states and buy its raw materials from fifteen more. It may sell its finished goods in every single state in the Union. It can still be chartered under just one state's law.

And even the smallest business is run on a national scale impossible in 1787. A factory started in Alabama may throw men out of work in Massachusetts, a thousand miles away. The price an Oregon farmer gets for wheat he sells in Chicago may cost an Oklahoma man his farm.

But big business and small business, says the Supreme Court, is nobody's business but the states'. In spite of the power the founding fathers meant for the national government, that government can not now interfere. And the

232

THE ORIGINAL CONSTITUTION

Preamble

We, the people of the United States, in order to form a more perfect union, establish justice, insure domestic tranquility, provide for the common defense, promote the general welfare, and secure the blessings of liberty to ourselves and our posterity, do ordain and establish this Constitution for the United States of America.

Article I

Section 1. All legislative powers herein granted shall be vested in a Congress of the United States, which shall consist of a Senate and House of Representatives.

Section 2. The House of Representatives shall be composed of members chosen every second year by the people of the several states, and the electors in each state shall have the qualifications requisite for electors of the most numerous branch of the state legislature.

No person shall be a representative who shall not have attained to the age of twenty-five years, and been seven years a citizen of the United States, and who shall not, when elected, be an inhabitant of that state in which he shall be chosen.

Representatives and direct taxes shall be apportioned among the several states which may be included within this Union, according to their respective numbers, which shall be determined by adding to the whole number of free persons, including those bound to service for a term of years, and excluding Indians not taxed, three-fifths of all other persons. The actual enumeration shall be made within three years after the first meeting of the Congress of the United States, and within every subsequent term of ten years, in such manner as they shall by law direct. The number of representatives shall not exceed one for every thirty thousand, but each state shall have at least one representative; and until such enumeration shall be made, the State of New Hampshire shall be entitled to choose three, Massachusetts eight, Rhode Island and Providence Plantations one, Connecticut five, New York six, New Jersey four, Pennsylvania eight, Delaware one, Maryland six, Virginia ten, North Carolina five, South Carolina five, and Georgia three.

When vacancies happen in the representation from any state, the executive authority thereof shall issue writs of election to fill such vacancies.

The House of Representatives shall choose their speaker and other officers; and shall have the sole power of impeachment.

SECTION 3. The Senate of the United States shall be composed of two senators from each state, chosen by the legislature thereof, for six years; and each senator shall have one vote.

Immediately after they shall be assembled in consequence of the first election, they shall be divided as equally as may be into three classes. The seats of the senators of the first class shall be vacated at the expiration of the second year, of the second class at the expiration of the fourth year, and of the third class at the expiration of the sixth year, so that one-third may be chosen every second year; and if vacancies happen by resignation, or otherwise, during the recess of the legislature of any state, the executive thereof may make temporary appointments until the next meeting of the legislature, which shall then fill such vacancies.

No person shall be a senator who shall not have attained to the age of thirty years, and been nine years a citizen of the United States, and who shall not, when elected, be an inhabitant of that state for which he shall be chosen.

The Vice-President of the United States shall be president of the Senate, but shall have no vote unless they be equally divided.

The Senate shall choose their other officers,

and also a president pro tempore, in the absence of the Vice-President, or when he shall exercise the office of President of the United States.

The Senate shall have the sole power to try all impeachments. When sitting for that purpose, they shall be on oath or affirmation. When the President of the United States is tried, the Chief Justice shall preside, and no person shall be convicted without the concurrence of two-thirds of the members present.

Judgment in cases of impeachment shall not extend further than to removal from office, and disqualification to hold and enjoy any office of honor, trust, or profit under the United States; but the party convicted shall nevertheless be liable and subject to indictment, trial, judgment, and punishment, according to law.

SECTION 4. The times, places, and manner of holding elections for senators and representatives shall be prescribed in each state by the legislature thereof; but the Congress may at any time by law make or alter such regulations, except as to the places of choosing senators.

The Congress shall assemble at least once in every year, and such meeting shall be on the first Monday in December, unless they shall by law appoint a different day.

SECTION 5. Each house shall be the judge of

the elections, returns, and qualifications of its own members, and a majority of each shall constitute a quorum to do business; but a smaller number may adjourn from day to day, and may be authorized to compel the attendance of absent members, in such manner and under such penalties as each house may provide.

Each house may determine the rules of its proceedings, punish its members for disorderly behavior, and, with the concurrence of two-thirds, expel a member.

Each house shall keep a journal of its proceedings, and from time to time publish the same, excepting such parts as may in their judgment require secrecy; and the yeas and nays of the members of either house on any question shall, at the desire of one-fifth of those present, be entered on the journal.

Neither house, during the session of Congress, shall, without the consent of the other, adjourn for more than three days, nor to any other place than that in which the two houses shall be sitting.

Section 6. The senators and representatives shall receive a compensation for their services, to be ascertained by law and paid out of the treasury of the United States. They shall in all cases, except treason, felony, and breach of the peace, be privileged from arrest during their attendance at the session of their respective houses, and in going to and returning from the same; and for any speech or debate in either house they shall not be questioned in any other place.

No senator or representative shall, during the time for which he was elected, be appointed to any civil office under the authority of the United States, which shall have been created, or the emoluments whereof shall have been increased during such time; and no person holding any office under the United States shall be a member of either house during his continuance in office.

SECTION 7. All bills for raising revenue shall originate in the House of Representatives; but the Senate may propose or concur with amendments as on other bills.

Every bill which shall have passed the House of Representatives and the Senate shall, before it become a law, be presented to the President of the United States; if he approve he shall sign it; but if not he shall return it, with his objections to that house in which it shall have originated, who shall enter the objections at large on their journal and proceed to reconsider it. If after such reconsideration two-thirds of that house shall agree to pass the bill, it shall be sent, together with the objections, to the other house, by which it shall likewise be reconsidered, and if

242

approved by two-thirds of that house, it shall become a law. But in all such cases the votes of both houses shall be determined by yeas and nays, and the names of the persons voting for and against the bill shall be entered on the journal of each house respectively. If any bill shall not be returned by the President within ten days (Sundays excepted) after it shall have been presented to him, the same shall be a law, in like manner as if he had signed it, unless the Congress by their adjournment prevent its return, in which case it shall not be a law.

Every order, resolution, or vote to which the concurrence of the Senate and House of Representatives may be necessary (except on a question of adjournment) shall be presented to the President of the United States; and before the same shall take effect, shall be approved by him, or being disapproved by him shall be repassed by two-thirds of the Senate and House of Representatives, according to the rules and limitations prescribed in the case of a bill.

SECTION 8. The Congress shall have power to lay and collect taxes, duties, imposts, and excises, to pay the debts, and provide for the common defense and general welfare of the United States; but all duties, imposts, and excises shall be uniform throughout the United States;

To borrow money on the credit of the United States;

To regulate commerce with foreign nations, and among the several states, and with the Indian tribes;

To establish an uniform rule of naturalization, and uniform laws on the subject of bankruptcies throughout the United States;

To coin money, regulate the value thereof and of foreign coin, and fix the standard of weights and measures;

To provide for the punishment of counterfeiting the securities and current coin of the United States;

To establish post offices and post roads;

To promote the progress of science and useful arts, by securing for limited times to authors and inventors the exclusive right to their respective writings and discoveries;

To constitute tribunals inferior to the Supreme Court;

To define and punish piracies and felonies committed on the high seas, and offenses against the law of nations;

To declare war, grant letters of marque and reprisal, and make rules concerning captures on land and water;

To raise and support armies, but no appropriation of money to that use shall be for a longer term than two years;

To provide and maintain a navy;

To make rules for the government and regulation of the land and naval forces;

To provide for calling forth the militia to execute the laws of the Union, suppress insurrections and repel invasions;

To provide for organizing, arming, and disciplining the militia, and for governing such part of them as may be employed in the service of the United States, reserving to the states respectively the appointment of the officers, and the authority of training the militia according to the discipline prescribed by Congress;

To exercise exclusive legislation in all cases whatsoever, over such district (not exceeding ten miles square) as may, by cession of particular states, and the acceptance of Congress, become the seat of the government of the United States, and to exercise like authority over all places purchased by the consent of the legislature of the state in which the same shall be, for the erection of forts, magazines, arsenals, dock yards, and other needful buildings;—and

To make all laws which shall be necessary and proper for carrying into execution the foregoing powers, and all other powers vested by this Con-

245

stitution in the government of the United States, or in any department or officer thereof.

SECTION 9. The migration or importation of such persons as any of the states now existing shall think proper to admit, shall not be prohibited by the Congress prior to the year one thousand eight hundred and eight, but a tax or duty may be imposed on such importation, not exceeding ten dollars for each person.

The privilege of the writ of habeas corpus shall not be suspended, unless when in cases of rebellion or invasion the public safety may require it.

No bill of attainder or ex post facto law shall be passed.

No capitation or other direct tax shall be laid, unless in proportion to the census or enumeration hereinbefore directed to be taken.

No tax or duty shall be laid on articles exported from any state.

No preference shall be given by any regulation of commerce or revenue to the ports of one state over those of another; nor shall vessels, bound to or from one state, be obliged to enter, clear, or pay duties in another.

No money shall be drawn from the treasury, but in consequence of appropriations made by law; and a regular statement and account of the receipts and expenditures of all public money shall be published from time to time.

No title of nobility shall be granted by the United States: and no person holding any office of profit or trust under them shall, without the consent of the Congress, accept of any present, emolument, office, or title of any kind whatever, from any king, prince, or foreign state.

SECTION 10. No state shall enter into any treaty, alliance, or confederation; grant letters of marque and reprisal; coin money; emit bills of credit; make anything but gold and silver coin a tender in payment of debts; pass any bill of attainer, ex post facto law, or law impairing the obligation of contracts, or grant any title of nobility.

No state shall, without the consent of the Congress, lay any imposts or duties on imports or exports, except what may be absolutely necessary for executing its inspection laws; and the net produce of all duties and imposts, laid by any state on imports or exports, shall be for the use of the treasury of the United States; and all such laws shall be subject to the revision and control of the Congress.

No state shall, without the consent of Congress, lay any duty of tonnage, keep troops or ships of war in time of peace, enter into any agreement or compact with another state, or with a foreign power, or engage in war, unless actually invaded or in such imminent danger as will not admit of delay.

ARTICLE II

SECTION 1. The executive power shall be vested in a President of the United States of America. He shall hold his office during the term of four years, and together with the Vice-President, chosen for the same term, be elected as follows:

Each state shall appoint, in such manner as the legislature thereof may direct, a number of electors equal to the whole number of senators and representatives to which the state may be entitled in the Congress; but no senator or representative, or person holding an office of trust or profit under the United States, shall be appointed an elector.

The electors shall meet in their respective states, and vote by ballot for two persons, of whom one at least shall not be an inhabitant of the same state with themselves. And they shall make a list of all the persons voted for, and of the number of votes for each; which list they shall sign and certify, and transmit sealed to the seat of the government of the United States, directed to the president of the Senate. The president of

248

the Senate shall, in the presence of the Senate and House of Representatives, open all the certificates, and the votes shall then be counted. The person having the greatest number of votes shall be the President, if such number be a majority of the whole number of electors appointed; and if there be more than one who have such majority, and have an equal number of votes, then the House of Representatives shall immediately choose by ballot one of them for President; and if no person have a majority, then from the five highest on the list the said House shall in like manner choose the President. But in choosing the President, the votes shall be taken by states, the representation from each state having one vote; a quorum for this purpose shall consist of a member or members from two-thirds of the states, and a majority of all the states shall be necessary to a choice. In every case, after the choice of the President, the person having the greatest number of votes of the electors shall be the Vice-President. But if there should remain two or more who have equal votes, the Senate shall choose from them by ballot the Vice-President.

The Congress may determine the time of choosing the electors, and the day on which they shall give their votes; which day shall be the same throughout the United States.

No person except a natural-born citizen, or a citizen of the United States at the time of the adoption of this Constitution shall be eligible to the office of President; neither shall any person be eligible to that office who shall not have attained to the age of thirty-five years, and been fourteen years a resident within the United States.

In case of the removal of the President from office, or of his death, resignation, or inability to discharge the powers and duties of the said office, the same shall devolve on the Vice-President, and the Congress may by law provide for the case of removal, death, resignation, or inability, both of the President and Vice-President, declaring what officer shall then act as President, and such officer shall act accordingly, until the disability be removed or a President shall be elected.

The President shall, at stated times, receive for his services, a compensation, which shall neither be increased nor diminished during the period for which he shall have been elected, and he shall not receive within that period any other emolument from the United States, or any of them.

Before he enter on the execution of his office, he shall take the following oath or affirmation: "I do solemnly swear (or affirm) that I will faithfully execute the office of President of the United States, and will to the best of my ability preserve, protect, and defend the Constitution of the United States."

SECTION 2. The President shall be commander in chief of the army and navy of the United States, and of the militia of the several states when called into the actual service of the United States; he may require the opinion, in writing, of the principal officer in each of the executive departments upon any subject relating to the duties of their respective offices, and he shall have power to grant reprieves and pardons for offenses against the United States, except in cases of impeachment.

He shall have power, by and with the advice and consent of the Senate, to make treaties, provided two-thirds of the senators present concur; and he shall nominate, and by and with the advice and consent of the Senate shall appoint ambassadors, other public ministers and consuls, judges of the Supreme Court, and all other officers of the United States whose appointments are not herein otherwise provided for, and which shall be established by law; but the Congress may by law vest the appointment of such inferior officers as they think proper in the President alone, in the courts of law, or in the heads of

251

departments.

The President shall have power to fill up all vacancies that may happen during the recess of the Senate, by granting commissions which shall expire at the end of their next session.

SECTION 3. He shall from time to time give to the Congress information of the state of the Union, and recommend to their consideration such measures as he shall judge necessary and expedient; he may, on extraordinary occasions, convene both houses, or either of them, and in case of disagreement between them, with respect to the time of adjournment, he may adjourn them to such time as he shall think proper; he shall receive ambassadors and other public ministers; he shall take care that the laws be faithfully executed, and shall commission all the officers of the United States.

SECTION 4. The President, Vice-President, and all civil officers of the United States shall be removed from office on impeachment for, and conviction of, treason, bribery, or other high crimes and misdemeanors.

ARTICLE III

SECTION 1. The judicial power of the United States shall be vested in one supreme court, and in such inferior courts as the Congress may from time to time ordain and establish. The judges, both of the supreme and inferior courts, shall hold their offices during good behavior, and shall, at stated times, receive for their services a compensation, which shall not be diminished during their continuance in office.

SECTION 2. The judicial power shall extend to all cases in law and equity arising under this Constitution, the laws of the United States, and treaties made, or which shall be made, under their authority; to all cases affecting ambassadors, other public ministers and consuls; to all cases of admiralty and maritime jurisdiction; to controversies to which the United States shall be a party; to controversies between two or more states; between a state and citizens of another state; between citizens of different states; between citizens of the same state claiming lands under grants of different states, and between a state, or the citizens thereof, and foreign states, citizens or subjects.

In all cases affecting ambassadors, other public ministers and consuls, and those in which a state shall be party, the Supreme Court shall have original jurisdiction. In all the other cases before mentioned, the Supreme Court shall have appellate jurisdiction, both as to law and fact, with such exceptions and under such regulations as the Congress shall make.

The trial of all crimes, except in cases of impeachment, shall be by jury; and such trial shall be held in the state where the said crimes shall have been committed; but when not committed within any state the trial shall be at such place or places as the Congress may by law have directed.

SECTION 3. Treason against the United States shall consist only in levying war against them or in adhering to their enemies, giving them aid and comfort. No person shall be convicted of treason unless on the testimony of two witnesses to the same overt act or on confession in open court.

The Congress shall have power to declare the punishment of treason, but no attainder of treason shall work corruption of blood or forfeiture, except during the life of the person attainted.

ARTICLE IV

SECTION 1. Full faith and credit shall be given in each state to the public acts, records, and judicial proceedings of every other state. And the Congress may by general laws prescribe the manner in which such acts, records, and proceedings shall be proved, and the effect thereof.

SECTION 2. The citizens of each state shall be entitled to all privileges and immunities of citi-

254

zens in the several states.

A person charged in any state with treason, felony, or other crime, who shall flee from justice and be found in another state, shall on demand of the executive authority of the state from which he fled be delivered up, to be removed to the state having jurisdiction of the crime.

No person held to service or labor in one state, under the laws thereof, escaping into another, shall, in consequence of any law or regulation therein, be discharged from such service or labor, but shall be delivered up on claim of the party to whom such service or labor may be due.

SECTION 3. New states may be admitted by the Congress into this Union; but no new state shall be formed or erected within the jurisdiction of any other state; nor any state be formed by the junction of two or more states, or parts of states, without the consent of the legislatures of the states concerned as well as of the Congress.

The Congress shall have power to dispose of and make all needful rules and regulations respecting the territory or other property belonging to the United States; and nothing in this Constitution shall be so construed as to prejudice any claims of the United States or of any particular state.

SECTION 4. The United States shall guarantee to every state in this Union a republican form of government, and shall protect each of them against invasion; and on application of the legislature or of the executive (when the legislature cannot be convened) against domestic violence.

ARTICLE V

The Congress, whenever two-thirds of both houses shall deem it necessary, shall propose amendments to this Constitution, or, on the application of the legislatures of two-thirds of the several states, shall call a convention for proposing amendments, which, in either case, shall be valid to all intents and purposes, as part of this Constitution, when ratified by the legislatures of three-fourths of the several states, or by conventions in three-fourths thereof, as the one or the other mode of ratification may be proposed by the Congress; provided, that no amendment which may be made prior to the year one thousand eight hundred and eight shall in any manner affect the first and fourth clauses in the ninth section of the first article; and that no state, without its consent, shall be deprived of its equal suffrage in the Senate.

ARTICLE VI

All debts contracted and engagements entered into before the adoption of this Constitution shall

256

be as valid against the United States under this Constitution as under the Confederation.

This Constitution, and the laws of the United States which shall be made in pursuance thereof; and all treaties made, or which shall be made, under the authority of the United States, shall be the supreme law of the land; and the judges in every state shall be bound thereby, anything in the Constitution or laws of any state to the contrary notwithstanding.

The Senators and Representatives before mentioned, and the members of the several state legislatures, and all executive and judicial officers, both of the United States and of the several states, shall be bound by oath or affirmation to support this Constitution; but no religious test shall ever be required as a qualification to any office or public trust under the United States.

ARTICLE VII

The ratification of the conventions of nine states shall be sufficient for the establishment of this Constitution between the states so ratifying the same.

257

THE TWENTY-SIX AMENDMENTS

Amendment I

Congress shall make no law respecting an establishment of religion, or prohibiting the free exercise thereof; or abridging the freedom of speech, or of the press, or the right of the people peaceably to assemble and to petition the government for a redress of grievances.

Amendment II

A well regulated militia being necessary to the security of a free state, the right of the people to keep and bear arms shall not be infringed.

Amendment III

No soldier shall in time of peace be quartered in any house without the consent of the owner, nor in time of war, but in a manner to be prescribed by law.

Amendment IV

The right of the people to be secure in their persons, houses, papers, and effects, against unreasonable searches and seizures, shall not be violated, and no warrants shall issue, but upon probable cause, supported by oath or affirmation, and particularly describing the place to be searched and the persons or things to be seized.

AMENDMENT V

No person shall be held to answer for a capital or otherwise infamous crime, unless on a presentment or indictment of a grand jury, except in cases arising in the land or naval forces, or in the militia, when in actual service in time of war or public danger; nor shall any person be subject for the same offense to be twice put in jeopardy of life or limb; nor shall be compelled in any criminal case to be a witness against himself, nor be deprived of life, liberty, or property, without due process of law; nor shall private property be taken for public use, without just compensation.

AMENDMENT VI

In all criminal prosecutions, the accused shall enjoy the right to a speedy and public trial by an impartial jury of the state and district wherein the crime shall have been committed, which district shall have been previously ascertained by law, and to be informed of the nature and cause of the accusation; to be confronted with the witnesses against him; to have compulsory process for obtaining witnesses in his favor, and to have the assistance of counsel for his defense.

Amendment VII

In suits at common law, where the value in controversy shall exceed twenty dollars, the right of trial by jury shall be preserved, and no fact tried by a jury shall be otherwise re-examined in any court of the United States, then according to the rules of the common law.

Amendment VIII

Excessive bail shall not be required, nor excessive fines imposed, nor cruel and unusual punishments inflicted.

Amendments IX

The enumeration in the Constitution of certain rights shall not be construed to deny or disparage others retained by the people.

Amendment X

The powers not delegated to the United States by the Constitution, nor prohibited by it to the states, are reserved to the states respectively, or to the people.

Amendment XI

The judicial power of the United States shall not be construed to extend to any suit in law or equity, commenced or prosecuted against one of the United States by citizens of another State, or by citizens or subjects of any foreign state.

AMENDMENT XII

The electors shall meet in their respective states and vote by ballot for President and Vice-President, one of whom at least shall not be an inhabitant of the same state with themselves; they shall name in their ballots the person voted for as President, and in distinct ballots the person voted for as Vice-President, and they shall make distinct lists of all persons voted for as President, and of all persons voted for as Vice-President, and of the number of votes for each, which lists they shall sign and certify, and transmit sealed to the seat of government of the United States, directed to the president of the Senate. The president of the Senate shall, in presence of the Senate and House of Representatives, open all the certificates, and the votes shall then be counted. The person having the greatest number of votes for President shall be the President, if such number be a majority of the whole number of electors appointed; and if no person have such majority, then from the persons having the highest numbers not exceeding three on the list of those voted for as President, the House of Representatives shall choose immediately, by ballot, the President. But in choosing the President, the votes shall be taken by states, the representation from each state having one vote; a quorum for this purpose shall consist of a member or members from two-thirds of the states, and a majority of all the states shall be necessary to a choice. And if the House of Representatives shall not choose a President whenever the right of choice shall devolve upon them, before the fourth day of March next following, then the Vice-President shall act as President, as in the case of the death or other constitutional disability of the President. The person having the greatest number of votes as Vice-President shall be the Vice-President, if such number be a majority of the whole number of electors appointed; and if no person have a majority, then from the two highest numbers on the list the Senate shall choose the Vice-President; a quorum for the purpose shall consist of two-thirds of the whole number of Senators, and a majority of the whole number shall be necessary to a choice. But no person constitutionally ineligible to the office of President shall be eligible to that of Vice-President of the United States.

AMENDMENT XIII

SECTION 1. Neither slavery nor involuntary servitude, except as a punishment for crime whereof the party shall have been duly convicted, shall exist within the United States or any place subject to their jurisdiction.

SECTION 2. Congress shall have power to enforce this article by appropriate legislation.

AMENDMENT XIV

SECTION 1. All persons born or naturalized in the United States, and subject to the jurisdiction thereof, are citizens of the United States and of the state wherein they reside. No state shall make or enforce any law which shall abridge the privileges or immunities of citizens of the United States; nor shall any state deprive any person of life, liberty, or property, without due process of law; nor deny to any person within its jurisdiction the equal protection of the laws.

SECTION 2. Representatives shall be apportioned among the several states according to their respective numbers, counting the whole number of persons in each state, excluding Indians not taxed. But when the right to vote at any election for the choice of electors for President and Vice-President of the United States, representatives in Congress, the executive and judicial officers of a state, or the members of the legislature thereof, is denied to any of the male inhabitants of such state, being twenty-one years of age and citizens of the United States, or in any way abridged, except for participation in rebellion, or other crime, the basis of representation therein shall be reduced in the proportion which the number of such male citizens shall bear to the whole number of male citizens twenty-one years of age in such state.

SECTION 3. No person shall be a senator or representative in Congress, or elector of President and Vice-President, or hold any office, civil or military, under the United States, or under any state, who, having previously taken an oath as a member of Congress, or as an officer of the United States, or as a member of any state legislature, or as an executive or judicial officer of any state, to support the Constitution of the United States, shall have engaged in insurrection or rebellion against the same, or given aid or comfort to the enemies thereof. But Congress may, by a vote of two-thirds of each house, remove such disability.

SECTION 4. The validity of the public debt of the United States, authorized by law, including debts incurred for payment of pensions and bounties for services in suppressing insurrection or rebellion, shall not be questioned. But neither the United States nor any state shall assume or pay any debt or obligation incurred in aid of insurrection or rebellion against the United States, or any claim for the loss or emancipation of any slave; but all such debts, obligations, and claims shall be held illegal and void.

SECTION 5. The Congress shall have power to enforce, by appropriate legislation, the provisions of this article.

AMENDMENT XV

SECTION 1. The right of citizens of the United States to vote shall not be denied or abridged by the United States or by any state on account of race, color, or previous condition of servitude.

SECTION 2. The Congress shall have power to enforce this article by appropriate legislation.

AMENDMENT XVI

The Congress shall have power to lay and collect taxes on incomes, from whatever source derived, without apportionment among the several states and without regard to any census or enumeration.

AMENDMENT XVII

The Senate of the United States shall be composed of two senators from each state, elected by the people thereof for six years; and each senator shall have one vote. The electors in each state shall have the qualifications requisite for electors of the most numerous branch of the state legislatures.

When vacancies happen in the representation of any state in the senate, the executive authority of such state shall issue writs of election to fill such vacancies; provided, that the legislature of any state may empower the executive thereof to make temporary appointments until the people fill the vacancies by election as the legislature may direct.

This amendment shall not be so construed as to affect the election or term of any senator chosen before it becomes valid as part of the Constitution.

AMENDMENT XVIII

SECTION 1. After one year from the ratification of this article the manufacture, sale, or transportation of intoxicating liquors within, the importation thereof into, or exportation thereof from the United States and all territory subject to the jurisdiction thereof, for beverage purposes is hereby prohibited.

SECTION 2. The Congress and the several states shall have concurrent power to enforce this article by appropriate legislation.

SECTION 3. This article shall be inoperative unless it shall have been ratified as an amendment to the Constitution by the legislatures of the several states, as provided in the Constitution, within seven years from the date of the submission hereof to the states by the Congress.

AMENDMENT XIX

The right of the citizens of the United States to vote shall not be denied or abridged by the United States or by any state on account of sex.

Congress shall have power to enforce this article by appropriate legislation.

AMENDMENT XX

SECTION 1. The terms of the President and Vice-President shall end at noon on the 20th Day of January, and the terms of senators and representatives at noon on the 3rd day of January, of the years in which such terms would have ended if this article had not been ratified; and the terms of their successors shall then begin.

SECTION 2. The Congress shall assemble at

least once in every year, and such meeting shall begin at noon on the 3rd day of January, unless they shall by law appoint a different day.

SECTION 3. If, at the time fixed for the beginning of the term of the President, the President elect shall have died, the Vice-President elect shall become President. If a President shall not have been chosen before the time fixed for the beginning of his term, or if the President elect shall have failed to qualify, then the Vice-President elect shall act as President until a President shall have qualified; and the Congress may by law provide for the case wherein neither a President elect nor a Vice-President elect shall have qualified, declaring who shall then act as President, or the manner in which one who is to act shall be selected, and such person shall act accordingly until a President or Vice-President shall have qualified.

SECTION 4. The Congress may by law provide for the case of the death of any of the persons from whom the House of Representatives may choose a President, whenever the right of choice shall have devolved upon them, and for the case of the death of any of the persons from whom the Senate may choose a Vice-President. whenever the right of choice shall have devolved upon them.

Section 5. Sections 1 and 2 shall take effect on the 15th day of October following the ratification of this article.

Section 6. This article shall be inoperative unless it shall have been ratified as an amendment to the Constitution by the legislatures of three-fourths of the several states within seven years from the date of its submission.

Amendment XXI

Section 1. The eighteenth article of amendment to the Constitution of the United States is hereby repealed.

Section 2. The transportation or importation into any state, territory, or possession of the United States, for delivery or use therein of intoxicating liquors, in violation of the laws thereof, is hereby prohibited.

Section 3. This article shall be inoperative unless it shall have been ratified as an amendment to the Constitution by conventions in the several states, as provided in the Constitution, within seven years from the date of the submission hereof to the states by the Congress.

AMENDMENT XXII

No person shall be elected to the office of the President more than twice, and no person who has held the office of President, or acted as President, for more than two years of a term to which some other person was elected President shall be elected to the office of the President more than once.

But this Article shall not apply to any person holding the office of President when this Article was proposed by the Congress, and shall not prevent any person who may be holding the office of President, or acting as President, during the term within which this Article becomes operative from holding the office of President or acting as President during the remainder of such term.

This article shall be inoperative unless it shall have been ratified as an amendment to the Constitution by the legislatures of three-fourths of the several states within seven years from the date of its submission to the states by the Congress.

AMENDMENT XXIII

SECTION 1. The District constituting the seat of Government of the United States shall appoint in such manner as the Congress may direct:

A number of electors of President and Vice-President equal to the whole number of Senators and Representatives in Congress to which the District would be entitled if it were a State, but in no event more than the least populous State; they shall be in addition to those appointed by the States, but they shall be considered, for the purposes of the election of President and Vice-President, to be electors appointed by a State; and they shall meet in the District and perform such duties as provided by the twelfth article of amendment.

SECTION 2.   The Congress shall have power to enforce this article by appropriate legislation.

AMENDMENT XXIV

SECTION 1.   The right of citizens of the United States to vote in any primary or other election for President or Vice President, for electors for President or Vice President, or for Senator or Representative in Congress, shall not be denied or abridged by the United States or any state by reason of failure to pay any poll tax or other tax.

SECTION 2.   The Congress shall have the power to enforce this article by appropriate legislation.

AMENDMENT XXV

SECTION 1.   In case of the removal of the President from office or of his death or resignation, the Vice President shall become President.

SECTION 2.   Whenever there is a vacancy in the office of the Vice President, the President shall nominate a Vice President who shall take office upon confirmation by a majority vote of both Houses of Congress.

SECTION 3. Whenever the President transmits to the President Pro Tempore of the Senate and the Speaker of the House of Representatives his written declaration that he is unable to discharge the powers and duties of his office, and until he transmits to them a written declaration to the contrary, such powers and duties shall be discharged by the Vice President as Acting President.

SECTION 4. Whenever the Vice President and a majority of either the principal officers of the executive departments or of such other body as Congress may by law provide, transmit to the President Pro Tempore of the Senate and the Speaker of the House of Representatives their written declaration that the President is unable to discharge the powers and duties of his office, the Vice President shall immediately assume the powers and duties of the office as Acting President.

Thereafter, when the President transmits to the President Pro Tempore of the Senate and the Speaker of the House of Representatives his written declaration that no inability exists, he shall resume the powers and duties of his office unless the Vice President and a majority of either the principal officers of the executive departments or of such other body as

Congress may by law provide, transmit within four days to the President Pro Tempore of the Senate and the Speaker of the House of Representatives their written declaration that the President is unable to discharge the powers and duties of his office. Thereupon Congress shall decide the issue, assembling within forty-eight hours for that purpose if not in session. If the Congress, within twenty-one days after receipt of the latter written declaration, or, if Congress is not in session, within twenty-one days after Congress is required to assemble, determines by two-thirds of both Houses that the President is unable to discharge the powers and duties of his office, the Vice President shall continue to discharge the same as Acting President; otherwise, the President shall resume the powers and duties of his office.

AMENDMENT XXVI

SECTION 1. The right of citizens of the United States, who are eighteen years of age or older, to vote shall not be denied or abridged by the United States or by any State on account of age.

SECTION 2. The Congress shall have power to enforce this article by appropriate legislation.

THE FIFTY-FIVE MEN

		Did he sign the Constitution?
Baldwin, Abraham	Georgia	Yes
Bassett, Richard	Delaware	Yes
Bedford, Gunning	Delaware	Yes
Blair, John	Virginia	Yes
Blount, William	North Carolina	Yes
Brearley, David	New Jersey	Yes
Broom, Jacob	Delaware	Yes
Butler, Pierce	South Carolina	Yes
Carroll, Daniel	Maryland	Yes
Clymer, George	Pennsylvania	Yes
Davie, William R.	North Carolina	No –
Dayton, Jonathan	New Jersey	Yes
Dickinson, John	Delaware	Yes
Ellsworth, Oliver	Connecticut	No –
Few, William	Georgia	Yes
Fitzsimons, Thomas	Pennsylvania	Yes
Franklin, Benjamin	Pennsylvania	Yes
Gerry, Elbridge	Massachusetts	No
Gilman, Nicholas	New Hampshire	Yes
Gorham, Nathaniel	Massachusetts	Yes
Hamilton, Alexander	New York	Yes
Houston, William	Georgia	No
Houston, William C.	New Jersey	No
Ingersoll, Jared	Pennsylvania	Yes
Jenifer, Daniel of St. Thomas	Maryland	Yes

		Did he sign the Constitution?
Johnson, William Samuel	Connecticut	Yes
King, Rufus	Massachusetts	Yes
Langdon, John	New Hampshire	Yes
Lansing, John	New York	No
Livingston, William	New Jersey	Yes
Madison, James	Virginia	Yes
Martin, Alexander	North Carolina	No
Martin, Luther	Maryland	No
Mason, George	Virginia	No
McClurg, James	Virginia	No
McHenry, James	Maryland	Yes
Mercer, John Francis	Maryland	No
Mifflin, Thomas	Pennsylvania	Yes
Morris, Gouverneur	Pennsylvania	Yes
Morris, Robert	Pennsylvania	Yes
Paterson, William	New Jersey	Yes
Pierce, William	Georgia	No
Pinckney, Charles	South Carolina	Yes
Pinckney, Charles Cotesworth	South Carolina	Yes
Randolph, Edmund	Virginia	No
Read, George	Delaware	Yes
Rutledge, John	South Carolina	Yes
Sherman, Roger	Connecticut	Yes
Spaight, Richard Dobbs	North Carolina	Yes

	Did he sign the Constitution?
Strong, Caleb ....Massachusetts ...No	
Washington, George ..Virginia ....Yes	
Williamson, Hugh ....North Carolina ..Yes	
Wilson, James ....Pennsylvania ....Yes	
Wythe, George ....Virginia ....No	
Yates, Robert ....New York ......No	

José

Francisco
Jesús
Thomas
Jorge
Scott
Emma
Janet
Caro
Wolf
Hussein
Irma
Joan
Lolo
Darren
Fiona
Shelly
Gus.